War Department US

Regulations governing commercial radio service between ship and shore stations

Inktank publishing

War Department US

Regulations governing commercial radio service between ship and shore stations

Inktank publishing, 2018

www.inktank-publishing.com

ISBN/EAN: 9783747768792

WAR DEPARTMENT — OFFICE OF THE CHIEF SIGNAL OFFICER

MANUAL No. 2-A

REGULATIONS GOVERNING COMMERCIAL RADIO SERVICE BETWEEN SHIP AND SHORE STATIONS UNITED STATES ARMY

1914

WASHINGTON
GOVERNMENT PRINTING OFFICE
1914

War Department,
Office of the Chief of Staff,
Washington, February 7, 1914.

The regulations incorporated in this manual are for the guidance of officers and men in control of Army radio stations, coast and transport, and of the operators thereof. In them are incorporated such special regulations as are necessary in view of the adherence of the United States Government to the International Radio Convention, London, 1912. They supersede all instructions issued prior to this date.

The methods of operation herein prescribed shall be followed without deviation.

In general the word "ship" is used to refer to a radio station on shipboard, and "station" to refer to a coast station. Occasionally the word "station" is used to denote any radio station, ship or coast. Its meaning, where so used, will be obvious from the context.

Except as directed in Chapter I of these regulations, all accounts, reports, and remittances of tolls collected on radiograms should be made in conformity with "Regulations for United States Military Telegraph Lines, Alaskan Cables, and Wireless Telegraph Stations, 1911" (Signal Corps Manual No. 2).

Electricians in charge or chief operators of all Army radio stations are cautioned that they will be held responsible for the thorough instruction of the operators under their charge in these regulations and for their compliance therewith.

By order of the Secretary of War.

Leonard Wood,
Major General, Chief of Staff.

CONTENTS.

CHAPTER I.

REPORTS. REMITTANCES. FORMS.

(Paragraphs 1 to 59.)

CHAPTER I.

REPORTS—REMITTANCES—FORMS.

LIMITED TO RADIO TRAFFIC.

1. The following regulations will govern the interchange of traffic and accounts between stations of the United States Army Radio Service and connecting radio stations (ship or coastal), domestic or foreign.

NOT TO SUPERSEDE EXISTING REGULATIONS.

2. These regulations are not to supersede the regulations now in effect governing the interchange of traffic with connecting land-line companies, and will apply only to the exchange of traffic between this service and connecting radio companies, and ship-to-shore and shore-to-ship traffic between stations of this service. In so far as practicable they will be supplemented by "Regulations for United States military telegraph lines, Alaskan cables, and wireless telegraph stations, 1911" (Signal Corps Manual No. 2).

AUDIT.

3. For the purpose of auditing accounts, reports, and remittances of the transport radio stations and reports from Army land stations covering messages exchanged with ship stations, Government or commercial, two zones are hereby established, namely, New York and Seattle.

NEW YORK ZONE.

4. The New York zone will include all United States Army radio stations (ship or coastal), authorized to handle commercial business (see par. 6) on the coast of or in the waters of the Atlantic Ocean and those waters naturally contiguous thereto and west of the Suez Canal. Reports and remittances, as indicated below, should be forwarded promptly at the end of each month to the department signal officer, Eastern Department, Army Building, New York City.

SEATTLE ZONE.

5. The Seattle zone will include all United States Army radio stations (ship or coastal) authorized to handle commercial business (see par. 6) on the coast of or in the waters of the Pacific, Indian, and Artic oceans and those waters naturally contiguous thereto and east of the Suez Canal. Reports and remittances should be forwarded

promptly at the end of each month to the officer in charge Washington-Alaska Military Cable & Telegraph System, Seattle, Wash., *except* that money orders, checks, etc., should be made payable to the order of the "Auditor, Washington-Alaska Military Cable & Telegraph System."

COMMERCIAL STATIONS.

6. Certain coast stations of the Army Radio Service were opened to commercial business by act of Congress of August 13, 1912, and the authority to open others, upon certain contingencies, was vested in the Secretary of War.

Under the provisions of this act Army transport radio stations and the following Army coast stations are now open to commercial business under the rules of the international convention, London, 1912:

Nome, Alaska	St. Michael, Alaska.
Kotlik, Alaska.	Petersburg, Alaska.
Wrangell, Alaska.	Corregidor, P. I.

SUBJECT TO THE INTERNATIONAL CONVENTION.

7. All stations, coast and ship, open to commercial business must conform strictly to the requirements of international convention (Appendix VI).

EXCHANGE OF TRAFFIC.

8. Commercial messages may be exchanged by Army transports and by Army coast stations open to commercial business with any ship, naval or commercial. Such messages may also be exchanged by Army transports with any naval coast station open to commercial business and with any coast station operated by a commercial company or by a foreign government for commercial purposes, or may be exchanged with other vessels of the United States Army Transport Service.

COAST STATION TO CONTROL.

9. A coast station which handles commercial business controls all radio communication in its vicinity (Article XXIX of the Convention, Appendix VI), and it is incumbent upon ships to recognize this control and not to interfere with the communications of such a station. Ships may communicate amongst themselves, if within range of a coast station, only on condition that they cause no interference with the business of that station. By using very low power, ships can accomplish this result. A ship *must* cease sending on demand from a coast station. Army coast stations must give precedence to ship-to-shore work and ship-to-ship work over that with other stations. Operators at Army coast stations shall report cases of interference by ships.

DUTIES OF ZONE OFFICERS.

AUDIT.

10. The department signal officer, Eastern Department, Army Building, New York City, and the officer in charge Washington-Alaska Military Cable and Telegraph System, Seattle, Wash., will receive and audit the monthly telegraph reports, covering the radio accounts of each station (ship or coastal) within their respective zones.

PAYMENTS TO RADIO COMPANIES.

11. The Zone officer will make settlement with connecting radio companies for all "other line" tolls falling to them and their respective land-line connections from ships or stations of the United States Army Radio Service.

12. All payments to "other lines" should be made from "other line" funds on hand *after* the receipt and audit of the reports and remittances from the Army stations concerned.

13. Receipts for such payments should be taken on the "Monthly abstract of amounts paid and receipted for by 'other lines'" (Form 118), which will be submitted as a voucher to the monthly "other line" account current (Form 102).

COLLECTIONS FROM RADIO COMPANIES.

14. The Zone officer will collect from radio companies all tolls falling to Army radio stations (ship or coastal) and their respective land-line connections within their zone.

15. All such tolls falling to a "this line" ship—i. e., tolls for messages transmitted direct to an Army transport from an "other line" radio station and for which the zone officer will not receive the usual operator's invoices, etc.—should be taken up on the "Monthly abstract of this line receipts" (Form 129), under the name of the company from which collected, and subdivided under the name of each transport to which they pertain. "Bill United States military telegraph lines against other lines" (Form 116), fully accomplished and agreeing with the entries on the abstract, should accompany the account current of the responsible officer in lieu of the operator's invoices.

16. All such tolls falling to a "this line" shore station—i. e., tolls for messages transmitted direct to an Army shore station from an "other line" radio station—will be taken up by the shore station concerned, as prescribed in Signal Corps Manual No. 2 for land-line transfer offices, the shore station invoicing his bill against "other lines" as cash pertaining to his station accounts. The instructions contained in this paragraph will also apply to all commercial messages received from Army transports, *except that credit will be taken* *on the station account current for tolls due from Army transports in lieu of invoices and Form 116, inasmuch as the tolls pertaining thereto will be included in the transport's reports and remittances to the zone officer.*

17. All such tolls falling to "other line" connecting companies should be taken up by the shore station as "other line" receipts and accounted for as prescribed for land-line transfer officers (Signal Corps Manual No. 2). The zone officer will dispose of this class of receipts as prescribed in paragraphs 11–13.

SETTLEMENT FOR OFFICIAL MESSAGES.

18. Settlement with "other lines" for official messages transferred to them will be made as prescribed in paragraphs 109–114. It is not thought that any messages of this class will be transmitted to an "other line" foreign company, but should such be the case the original messages should be forwarded by the zone officer to the Chief Signal Officer of the Army for settlement of foreign company's charges.

REPORTS FROM ZONE OFFICERS.

19. No special reports covering radio traffic will be required from zone officers. The usual reports pertaining to telegraph line receipts, as now prescribed by Signal Corps Manual No. 2 and Army Regulations, will be submitted in the same form as heretofore and be inclusive of the radio accounts as indicated above.

REPORTS FROM SHORE STATIONS.

SUPPLEMENTARY REPORTS.

20. In addition to the regular station telegraph reports, as now prescribed by Signal Corps Manual No. 2, Army shore stations will also submit the following supplementary reports covering the radio traffic exchanged with ships at sea and connecting radio companies.

FORM NO. 156.

21. The "Abstract of commercial radio messages received and sent forward" (Form 156) is for use at shore stations *only*.

22. It should be a complete record of all commercial radio transactions during the month, *exclusive of radiograms filed locally*, and is supplementary to the monthly station telegraph accounts.

23. For the purpose of facilitating the audit and exchange of accounts between the zone officer and connecting radio companies it has been so arranged as to divide the traffic into two classes, i. e., OUTGOING and INCOMING.

24. A complete description of each *outgoing* and *incoming* message should be entered in columns 1 to 9 in the order of its transmission.

OUTGOING MESSAGES.

25. Outgoing messages are those coming to the station from the land line, interior radio stations, and other radio stations, Army or otherwise, and transmitted to ships at sea or connecting radio companies, as follows:

(*a*) Land line to ships.
(*b*) Land line to naval radio.
(*c*) Naval radio to ships.
(*d*) Army radio to ships.
(*e*) Army radio to naval radio (relayed).

Tolls due to "other line" on *outgoing* messages should be entered under the name of the "other line" company, using columns 11 to 15 (Form 156) for this purpose.

26. Messages of the subdivision indicated by letters (*a*), (*b*), (*d*), and (*e*) will be taken up by office of origin (or office where it first reaches "this line") in the check report (Form 105), which will enter the same opposite the name of the first "this line" shore station *via* which it was transmitted to ships at sea or "other line" radio companies. The shore station will check offices of origin in a corresponding manner.

27. Messages of the subdivision indicated by the letter (*c*) will be taken into the shore station's accounts in the same manner as similar messages filed locally. They will be entered on the check report opposite the name of the ship (whether to a "this" or "other" line ship) to which they were transmitted. Messages of this class transmitted to Army transports, as well as those described in the preceding paragraph, will be entered on the ship station's abstract of messages received.

INCOMING MESSAGES.

28. Incoming messages are those received at the shore station from ships at sea, Army or otherwise, or connecting radio companies and transmitted to the land lines or other radio shore stations, as follows:

(*a*) Ships to land line.
(*b*) Naval radio to land line.
(*c*) Ships to naval radio.
(*d*) Ships to Army radio.
(*e*) Naval radio to Army radio (relayed).

Tolls due to "other lines" on *incoming* messages should be entered under the name of the next connecting company to which the message is transferred, viz, "War Dept.," "W. U.," etc., using columns 16 to 20 for this purpose.

29. Messages of this class will be checked by the "this line" office of destination (or office where it is transferred to a connecting line for further transmission) against the shore station from whom received in the same manner as with messages originating at the shore station. The shore station will enter the same on the check report with the office of destination in the same manner as with similar messages filed locally on which tolls are collected. The shore station will forward with the monthly reports "Bill United States military telegraph lines against other lines" to cover all such tolls taken into the station accounts. The same will be invoiced as cash as prescribed in Signal Corps Manual No. 2. The instruction contained in this paragraph will also apply to all commercial messages received from Army transports, *except that credit will be taken on the station account current for tolls due from Army transports in lieu of invoices and Form 116, inasmuch as the tolls pertaining thereto will be included in the transport's reports and remittances to the zone officer.*

30. Under column 21 (Form 156) should be entered the total amount due to, or from, connecting lines and radio stations on *incoming* and *outgoing* messages.

31. Under columns 22 to 28 (Form 156) should be entered the total amount due from "other lines" including all station and land line charges, also total amount due from land lines including station charge.

32. Under column 29 (Form 156) enter name of any miscellaneous connecting company, not otherwise provided with a special column, with which traffic has been exchanged, also any notations relative to prepaid replies or any other information not covered by the foregoing.

33. Relayed messages coming within the provisions of paragraphs 275–280 are not to be taken into the station's monthly accounts nor checked with the stations concerned. In this respect they will be treated as any other relayed message in the manner customary on the land lines.

FORM 157.

34. This form "Abstract of messages accepted from the public and charges paid" (Form 157) is for use at shore stations only.

35. It should be a complete record of all radio transactions at shore stations, *exclusive of radiograms in transit and covered by Form 156* and is supplementary to the monthly station telegraph reports.

36. All tolls collected falling to shore or ship stations of the Army should be entered under column 8 of this form and taken into the station's account in the usual manner. Entry on the check report of all such messages will be with the ship or station of destination, Army or otherwise.

36a. All tolls collected falling to shore or ship stations of connecting companies should be entered under columns 9 to 12 of this form and taken into the station's account as "other line" receipts in the usual manner and as indicated in the preceding paragraph.

37. Invoices, receipts, and statement of remittances to cover all such tolls collected will be forwarded in the manner prescribed in Signal Corps Manual No. 2.

REPORTS FROM SHIP STATIONS.

SUPPLEMENTARY REPORTS.

38. In addition to the usual telegraph reports, as now prescribed by Signal Corps Manual No. 2, ship stations will also submit the following supplementary reports covering their radio transactions.

FORM 153.

39. The "Abstract of commercial messages accepted and charges paid" (Form 153) is for use at ship stations only.

40. In preparing monthly telegraph reports operators at ship stations should bear in mind that this form is a substitution for the usual check report (Form 105) in use on the land lines.

41. The headings under columns 1 to 7 are self-explanatory and should be carefully followed.

42. All tolls falling to the ship station should be entered under column 8 and taken up on the "this line" account current (Form 103) and remitted as "this line" tolls.

43. Likewise all tolls entered under columns 9 to 12 should be taken up on the "other line" account current (Form 104) and remitted as "other line" tolls.

44. Remittances of all radio receipts should be made as prescribed in Signal Corps Manual No. 2.

45. The originals of all messages should be forwarded with the reports to which they pertain.

FORM 154.

46. The form "Abstract of official messages accepted on which no tolls were collected" (Form 154) is for use at ship stations only.

47. This form should be used in connection with all official messages transmitted.

48. The original messages, properly certified and bearing indication on the face as to connecting company to which "other line" charges will fall, should accompany this report.

49. Settlement with connecting companies for "other line" charges will be made as prescribed in paragraphs 109–114.

FORM 155.

50. This form should be a complete description of all commercial messages received and delivered or relayed by ship stations.

51. A copy of all messages covered thereby should accompany this report.

TARIFF.

52. All data relative to charges, refunds, and rates will be found at the end of Chapter II.

BLANK FORMS.

53. The following enumerated forms will be used in connection with radio work and will be issued on requisition to the respective zone officers:

31-B. Message envelopes.
102. Account current "other line receipts" officer.
103. Account current "this line receipts" station.
104. Account current "other line receipts" station.
105. Check report.
116. Bill United States military telegraph lines against "other lines" operator.
118. Monthly statement of amount paid and receipted for by other lines.
121. Invoices of "...... line" tolls transferred, operator.
122. Receipt for "...... line" tolls (original and duplicate).
123-E. Telegrams, sent (station).
125-E. Telegrams, received (station).
125-F. Telegrams, official, sent, received, or relayed (station).
129. Abstract of "this line" receipts (zone officer).
132-A. Statement of remittances "this line."
132-B. Statement of remittances "other lines."
138. Operator's number sheet.
150. Radio operator's receipt to customer for tolls paid (station).
153. Abstract of COMMERCIAL messages accepted and charges paid (ship stations).
154. Abstract of OFFICIAL messages accepted on which no tolls were collected (ship stations).
155. Abstract of all COMMERCIAL messages received and delivered on board or relayed (ship stations).
156. Abstract of all COMMERCIAL radio messages received and sent forward (shore stations).
157. Abstract of messages accepted and charges paid (shore stations).

INFORMATION TO BE FORWARDED TO THE ZONE OFFICER.

54. In addition to filling out and forwarding the various forms required in the accounting work of radio stations, ship and shore, as given above, the following instructions shall be carried out at all such stations:

55. Every message carrying tolls or charges shall be given a serial number, additional to the regular sending or receiving number on it. This additional number is known as the SRS number, and is used in accounting only. The SRS number is not transmitted by radio or by telegraph, but is written on each copy made of each message. *Every* message handled by radio at an army radio station is given an SRS number by that station, whether the message is one received, relayed, or transmitted. The series of SRS numbers is continuous, and does not start afresh each day or month. Relayed messages have the capital letter "R" added to the SRS number; thus, SRS102R.

56. When service messages are sent concerning a message, such service messages shall be given the SRS number of the message to which they refer, followed by "a" for the first service, "b" for the second, and so on. Paid service messages are not numbered in this manner, but have separate numbers the same as regular commercial messages.

57. As is apparent from the above instructions, one and the same message will bear different SRS numbers at the various stations handling it.

FORWARDING OF COPIES OF MESSAGES.

58. The originals of all messages carrying tolls or charges showing all the information available, handled on any day by any station, shall be forwarded with the monthly reports. Duplicates shall be retained in the station's files. These copies must be fully filled out, showing all items in preamble as well as the message proper.

59. The originals forwarded and the duplicates in the station's files shall show any discrepancy in the counting of words; any delays exceeding one hour and the causes therefor; the charges collected, if any; also any other information which might be of use—as, for instance, the failure to obtain acknowledgment of receipt.

59a. In case a message is received from the land lines or other radio stations for transmission to a ship at sea, not within range (unless it has already passed the station), the message is to be held eight days. (See paragraphs 267–271.) In this case such message is not reported until—

(*a*) It is transmitted by radio; or

(*b*) The eight days have elapsed and notice of nondelivery sent.

29732°—14——2

CHAPTER II.

CHARGES. REFUNDS. RATES.

(Paragraphs 60 to 104.)

CHAPTER II.

CHARGES—REFUNDS—RATES.

CHARGES.

PLAIN COMMERCIAL MESSAGES.

60. *All* messages must be prepaid, and no collect commercial message shall be accepted, *except:*

1. When destined for points on the Washington-Alaska Military Cable & Telegraph System or for points on the line of a commercial company whose line directly connects with the military line, and which company has agreed in writing to the understanding prescribed in paragraph "*b*," rule 7, Signal Corps Manual No. 2; provided that the transmission of the message involves no telegraph, wireless, or cable companies who are not parties to the agreement specified above.

2. When message is in answer to a prepaid message the sender of which has made satisfactory deposit to cover reply.

3. Cases of emergency or where delay of transmission might imperil life.

4. Where the station transmitting the message belongs to some radiotelegraph company which has previously made satisfactory arrangements with the officer in charge at Seattle, guaranteeing the payment of tolls on such messages.

5. Where satisfactory arrangements have been made with the officer in charge at Seattle by the sender or company such person may represent, guaranteeing the payment of tolls involved by such message.

61. Charges are computed by adding together the various separate rates per word needed for ship radio charge, coast station radio charge, and land-line telegraph or cable charge between coast station and the inland telegraph office concerned. These various rates are given, so far as possible, at the end of this chapter. Should a rate be required for a point not listed herein, the operator shall consult the rate book of the Western Union Telegraph Co. or the Postal Telegraph-Cable Co. or, if necessary, send a service message to ascertain the rate.

62. The radio rate for stations of the United States Army Radio Service (ship or coastal) is five (5) cents per word, 10-word minimum.

63. The charge, where the radio service is performed wholly between transport and Army shore stations or between transport and transport will be the radio charge of five (5) cents per word, which will fall to the station or ship of origin as "this line" tolls.

64. Having arrived at the rate per word for transmission over the entire distance involved, the charge for the message is determined by multiplying the rate per word by the number of words in the message, determined according to the rules given in Chapter IV.

NOTE.—At present there is a 10-word minimum charge for radio transmission, both ship and coast station, and for land telegraph transmission. Therefore, if a message contains less than 10 words, a 10-word charge *must* be made for radio and land-line transmission. The 10-word minimum does not apply in computing foreign cable and incidental land-line charges on messages addressed to foreign points. (See example (f), par. 70.)

EXAMPLES.

(Rates indicated for other lines are subject to change.)

Ship to Land Lines (via Marconi).

65. (*a*) Charges on a radiogram from a ship approaching San Francisco, Cal., addressed to Chicago, Ill., would comprise the following:

	Cents.
Ship charge	5
Marconi charge	6
Western Union (or Postal)	8
Total charge per word	19

The charge for a message of 10 words, *or less*, would, therefore, be $1.90 and 19 cents for each additional word in excess of 10, address and signature counted. (See Chapter IV for rules on the counting of words.) 50 cents "this line," $1.40 "other lines."

Ship to Land Lines (via Army Radio Station).

66. (*b*) On a message addressed as above, the charges would comprise the following:

	Cents.
Ship charge	5
Western Union (or Postal)	8
Total charge per word	13

The charges for a message of 10 words, *or less*, would, therefore, be $1.30 and 13 cents for each additional word in excess of 10.

Ship to Land Lines (via Naval Radio Station).

67. (*c*) Same as shown for a Marconi station.

Ship to Land Lines and Foreign Points (via Marconi).

68. (*d*) Were the message cited in example (*a*) addressed to London, England, instead of to Chicago, Ill., the charges would then comprise the following:

	Cents.
Ship charge	5
Marconi charge	6
Western Union (exact number of words in the message)	37

The ship and shore radio charges are computed on a 10-word minimum basis. *The Western Union charge is based on the exact number of words in the message without regard to a 10-word minimum.* Therefore if the message cited contained only 6 words the total charge would be: Ship charge, 50 cents (10 words); Marconi charge,

60 cents (10 words); Western Union charge, $2.22 (six words); or a total of $3.32 for the message.

Ship to the United States (via Alaskan Army Radio Station).

69. (*e*) Charges on a radiogram from a ship approaching Nome, Alaska, addressed to Washington, D. C., would comprise the following:

	Cents.
Ship charge	5
Signal Corps (Nome–Seattle)	38
Western Union (Seattle–Washington)	10
Total charge per word	53

The charge for a 10-word message, *or less*, would therefore be $5.30 and 53 cents for each additional word in excess of 10.

NOTE.—*The method of computing Western Union charge for the exact number of words, as shown in example (d), does not apply to messages destined to offices of commercial companies in the United States and Canada.*

Ship to Foreign Points (via Alaskan Army Radio Station).

70. (*f*) Were the message cited in example (*e*) addressed to London, England, instead of to Washington, D. C., the charge would then comprise the following:

	Cents.
Ship charge	5
Signal Corps (Nome–Seattle) (exact number of words)	30
Western Union (Seattle–London)	37

The ship charge is computed on a 10-word minimum basis. The Signal Corps and Western Union charge is based on the exact number of words in the cablegram without regard to a 10-word minimum. Therefore if this message contained only six words the charge would be: Ship charge, 50 cents (10 words); Signal Corps, $1.80 (six words); Western Union, $2.22 (six words); or a total of $4.52 for the message.

Ship to the United States (via Alaska Naval Radio Station).

71. (*g*) Charges on a radiogram from a ship approaching the Sitka naval radio station, addressed to Washington, D. C., routed "via Signal Corps," would comprise the following:

	Cents.
Ship charge	5
Navy charge	5
Signal Corps (Sitka–Seattle)	16
Western Union (Seattle–Washington)	10
Total charge per word	36

The charge for a 10-word message would therefore be $3.60. (See par. 101 for an alternative route on messages of this class.)

From Ship to Ship (both being Army Stations).

71a. (*h*) On a message filed on board an Army transport, addressed to another Army transport within range, the charge will be the radio charge of 5 cents per word, 10-word minimum, which will fall to the ship of origin as "this line" tolls. The ship of destination will make no charge.

NOTE.—If the ship of destination is not within range and it becomes necessary to relay the message through another station (ship or coastal) the tolls falling to the relaying station should also be collected and reported, except as provided in paragraphs 275-280.

From Ship to Ship (one only being an Army Station).

71b. (*i*) On a message filed on an Army transport, addressed to a ship of another radio company, the charge will be the radio charge of 5 cents per word, plus the ship charge of the ship of destination, plus relaying charges as indicated in the preceding example.

VIA CORREGIDOR, P. I.

From Ship to Manila, P. I., via Corregidor, P. I., Shore Station.

71c. (*j*) On a message *from an Army transport* approaching Manila, addressed to Manila and transmitted through the Corregidor Army radio station, the charge will be the radio charge of 5 cents per word, 10-word minimum, which will fall to the ship of origin as "this line" tolls. No charge will be made to cover the Signal Corps cable service between Corregidor and Manila.

From Ship to Points in the Philippine Islands, beyond Manila, via Corregidor and Land Lines.

71d. (*k*) Were the message cited in example (*j*) addressed to a land-line station in the Province of Batangas, instead of to Manila, the charge would then comprise the following:

	Cents.
Ship charge (10-word minimum)	5
Land line (Manila-Batangas) (10-word minimum, address and signature not counted), for the message	40

The charges for a message *containing seven words in the text* and eight words in the address and signature, or a total of 15 words, radio count, would therefore be: Ship charge, 75 cents (15 words); land line, 40 cents (10-word message).

NOTE.—It will be necessary for the ship of origin to double check messages of this description, e. g., this message would be checked 15/7, the first group indicating the ship count and the second group the land-line count.

From Ship to Points in the Philippine Islands, beyond Manila, via Corregidor and Commercial Cable.

71e. (*l*) Were the message cited above addressed to the town of Iloilo, instead of to Manila, the charge would then comprise the following, *if routed via Commercial Cable:*

	Cents.
Ship charge	5
Cable charge (Manila-Iloilo) (exact number of words, cable count)	15

The charges for a message similar to that cited in example (*k*) would therefore be: Ship charge, 75 cents (15 words); cable charge, $2.25 (15 words); or a total of $3 for the message.

NOTE.—All of the foregoing examples will also apply to messages transmitted from ship stations of *other* radio companies, or from shore to ships, transport or otherwise, except that the shore charge of 5 cents per word will be substituted for the "this line" ship charge.

71f. The Corregidor station will render complete reports to Seattle as prescribed for shore stations. (See Chap. I.)

72. In connection with the foregoing examples it should be noted that the cable count, 10-word minimum, is always used in computing radio and land-line charges on messages destined for Alaska, United States, and Canada via Alaskan stations.

73. The 10-word minimum does not apply in computing *foreign cable and intervening land-line charges* on messages addressed to foreign points. (See example (*f*) par. 70.)

SPECIAL TYPES OF RADIOGRAMS.

Answer Prepaid.

Abbreviated Designation "RP....."

74. Charges are computed in the same manner as for paid messages carrying the same check, plus the added amount to prepay a reply, as noted in the preamble and address. The 10-word minimum applies to the return message in the same manner as to the original. Example: A 10-word message filed on an Army vessel, sent via Marconi station at Charleston, S. C., addressed to Chicago, would have the ship charge of 5 cents, the Marconi charge of 6 cents, and the land line of 6 cents, total charge per word, 17 cents, or $1.70 for 10 words; and if the sender desired a prepaid reply of 10 words, he would pay $3.40 on this message and the special prefix would be "RP–1.70." The amount paid for the reply should be taken up as "other line" tolls.

75. Senders of "Answer prepaid" messages should be advised that the amount paid for a reply is virtually a remittance to the addressee, who can, if he should so desire, use the reply certificate in payment, or part payment, for tolls on a message to another addressee at another destination. Prepayment therefore does not guarantee that the addressee will be restricted in his use of a reply certificate to a reply to any particular message. (See par. 127.)

Radiograms Calling for Repetition of Message.

Abbreviated Designation "TC."

76. Charges are computed in the same manner as for a paid message carrying the same check, plus one-fourth additional. Example: A 10-word message from an Army vessel, via Marconi, Charleston to Chicago, is $1.70. Hence, a repeat-back message over this route would cost $1.70 plus 43 cents, or a total of $2.13.

Radiograms to be Delivered by Mail.

Abbreviated Designation "Post" or "PR."

77. Charges are computed in the same manner as for a paid message carrying the same check, to the point where message is to be mailed, plus 5 cents for postage. The amount collected for postage falls to the ship or station making the expenditure.

Special Delivery Radiograms.

Designation "Express."

78. Charges are the same as for a paid radiogram carrying the same check. Note that the addressee pays for special delivery. Example: Ship to Glen Echo, Md., via Marconi, Charleston, S. C., would have charges as follows: Ship, 5 cents; station, 6 cents; plus land-line rate from Charleston to Washington, D. C., 6 cents=equals 17 cents per word, or a total of $1.70.

NOTE.—Addressee would pay the charge for a special messenger to deliver this message from Washington, D. C. to Glen Echo, Md. The sender, whenever practicable, should indicate in the address of the message the nearest telegraph office.

Multiple Radiograms.

Abbreviated Designation "TMx."

80. Charges are calculated in two parts, as follows: First, the radio transmission charge (ship and coast station) is the same as that of a paid message carrying the same check; second, land-line and cable charge on each message forwarded. Note that the radiogram starts as a multiple message, *i. e.*, more than one address or more than one addressee and but one text, but is placed on land line broken up into as many separate messages as there are addresses or addressees, each message being a unit. Example: A multiple message carrying a check of 20 words filed on the U. S. S. WYOMING, sent via Jupiter, addressed to Tom James, 60 South Street, and Wiley Nelson, 80 Monroe Street, New Orleans, would have, first, a station charge for 20 words, *i. e.*, 20 × 6c. = $1.20, and, second, a land-line charge on two messages of 13 words each, *i. e.*, 13 × 5c. = 65c., and 13 × 5c. = 65c. Explanatory: The special prefix "TMx" is dropped in placing this message on the land line, and on the first message the following words are dropped in the address—"and Wiley Nelson, 80 Monroe Street"—hence seven words are dropped. Likewise, on the second message, to Nelson, seven words would be dropped. Consequently, each land-line message would contain a 13-word check. Total charges = $1.20 + 65c. + 65c. = $2.50.

Radiograms Calling for Acknowledgment of Receipt.

Abbreviated Designation "PC" or "PCP."

(This type applies only to messages originating on shore.)

81. *On "PCP" messages* the charge is the same as for a paid message carrying the same check, plus charge of five-word message from coast station to office of origin.

NOTE.—By this five-word message the coast station informs the telegraph office of origin of the hour and date of transmitting message to ship.

82. *On "PC" messages* the charge is the same as on a paid message carrying the same check, the mail acknowledgment being sent free by the coast station.

Paid Service Notices.

Prefix "RADIO ST."

83. Charge same as for a paid message carrying the same check, the charge being for the number of words necessary for service message (10-word minimum applies). There is no charge for address or signature, as none is sent.

"Ocean Letters" or Radiograms Transmitted to a Ship to be Mailed at a Port of Call.

Special Designation "Poste" or "Mail."

84. Same charges as for a paid message carrying the same check, plus 5c. necessary for postage in mailing message.

Counting of Supplementary Instructions.

85. On all special types of messages the abbreviated supplementary instructions are counted as one word and included in the check and charge. For example: "RP 1.80," "Express." However, if these instructions are spelled out in full, each word counts in the check and is charged for. Example: "Acknowledgment prepaid" should be checked as two words.

Relayed Messages.

86. All ships or shore stations relaying a commercial message are entitled to their regular charge. If the message which is relayed originates on board a ship, the ship or coast station which does the relaying charges the ship of origin with the cost of relaying; whereas, if the message originates on shore, the ship of destination is chargeable with the relaying. The U. S. Army, also the Naval Radio Service, make no charge for relaying commercial messages. Certain of the commercial companies likewise make no charge for this service. The Marconi Wireless Telegraph Co. is one which does not make the charge. (See pars. 275–280.)

REFUNDS.

87. Requests for refund of charges paid on radiograms should be addressed to the zone officer, except as noted below.

88. Refunds are not in order on account of the nondelivery of a radiogram due to such reasons as "Addressee unknown," "Addressee deceased," "Addressee not aboard ship," "Addressee left town," and similar causes.

EXCEPTION.—The ship or station of origin may refund charges collected on a radiogram direct to the sender *only* when the ship or station is unable to get the message in question to the next common carrier, or when a service message is received stating the inability of another common carrier to get the message through to its destination, on account of the breakdown of some system, such as cable down, land line down, ship out of range, etc.

Receipt to be given the addressee of an answer-prepaid message when received aboard ship.

89. No......

U. S. A. T .... (date) .... 191 .

Due .... the sum of $........, on account of SRS No. ...., which may be used in payment of charges on radiograms filed at this station by him within forty-two days from this date. Thereafter this receipt is void.

Accepted in payment of charges on SRS No. ....

....

U. S. Army.

90. When an answer-prepaid message (abbreviated designation "RP..") is received aboard ship, the person authorized to collect charges due on radiograms should give the person who received an answer-prepaid message a receipt, made out in accordance with the form above, said receipt calling for the amount prepaid for reply.

91. This receipt is to be numbered serially for each month, and a duplicate copy of the same forwarded to the zone officer attached to the SRS message which authorizes the issuance of this receipt.

92. If this receipt is presented within 42 days from the date it is issued it should be accepted in payment of charges on commercial messages, and should be forwarded to the zone officer and invoiced as cash, together with the other moneys collected for charges during the month in which the receipt is taken up. (See pars. 122–127.)

RATES.

93. TABLE A.—*Telegraph and cable rates to points in the United States, Canada, and Mexico from United States naval radio stations.*

(Rates quoted do not include the radio charges, which must be added.)

	Charleston, S. C.	St. Augustine, Jupiter Inlet, and Pensacola, Fla.	Key West, Fla.	Guantanamo Bay. C. F. des C. T.	Guantanamo Bay. C. & S. A. T. Co.	San Juan, P. R.	Colon, I. C. Z. W. I. & P. T. Co.	Balboa, I. C. Z. C. & S. A. T. Co.	Tatoosh Island, Wash.	North Head, Wash.	Cape Blanco, Oreg.	Eureka, Point Arguello, and San Diego, Cal.	Guam.
Station radio rate	$0.05	$0.05	$0.05	$0.05		$0.05	$0.05		$0.05	$0.05	$0.05	$0.05	$0.05
Alabama	.05	.05	.09	.20	.22	.50	.46	.48	.11	.10	.12	.10	.94
Alberta	.10	.10	.14	.25	.32	.55	.62	.64	.07	.06	.08	.08	......
Arizona	.10	.10	.14	.25	.28	.55	.50	.52	.09	.08	.10	.06	.89
Arkansas	.06	.05	.09	.25	.25	.55	.49	.51	.11	.10	.12	.10	.94
British Columbia	.10	.10	.14	.25	.32	.55	62.	.64	.06	.05	.07	.06	.93
California	.10	.10	.14	.25	.28	.55	.50	.52	.07	.06	.07	.03	.89
Colorado	.08	.08	.12	.25	.25	.55	.49	.51	.09	.08	.10	.08	.91
Connecticut	.06	.06	.10	.20	.19	.50	.43	.45	.11	.10	.12	.10	.97
Delaware	.05	.06	.10	.20	.19	.50	.43	.45	.11	.10	.12	.10	.97
District of Columbia	.05	.06	.10	.20	.19	.50	.43	.45	.11	.10	.12	.10	.97
Florida (except Key West)	.05	.04	.04	.20	.25	.50	.49	.51	.11	.10	.12	.10	.97
Key West	.09	.04	......	.20	.25	.50	.49	.51	.15	.14	.16	.14	.97
Georgia	.05	.05	.09	.20	.22	.50	.46	.48	.11	.10	.12	.10	.97
Idaho	.10	.10	.14	.25	.28	.55	.50	.52	.06	.05	.07	.06	.89
Illinois	.06	.06	.10	.20	.22	.50	.46	.48	.09	.08	.10	.08	.94

TABLE A.—*Telegraph and cable rates to points in the United States, Canada, and Mexico from United States naval radio stations*—Continued.

	Charleston, S. C.	St. Augustine, Jupiter Inlet, and Pensacola, Fla.	Key West, Fla.	Guantanamo Bay. C. F. des C. T.	Guantanamo Bay. C. & S. A. T. Co.	San Juan, P. R.	Colon, I. C. Z. W. I. & P. T. Co.	Balboa, I. C. Z. C. & S. A. T. Co.	Tatoosh Island, Wash.	North Head, Wash.	Cape Blanco, Oreg.	Eureka, Point Arguello, and San Diego, Cal.	Guam.
Indiana	$0.06	$0.06	$0.10	$.20	.22	$0.50	$.46	.48	$0.11	$0.10	$0.12	$0.10	$0.94
Iowa	.06	.06	.10	.25	.25	.55	.49	.51	.09	.08	.10	.08	.94
Kansas	.08	.08	.12	.25	.25	.55	.49	.51	.09	.08	.10	.08	.91
Kentucky	.05	.05	.09	.20	.22	.50	.46	.48	.11	.10	.12	.10	.94
Louisiana	.05	.05	.09	.20	.25	.55	.45	.47	.11	.10	.12	.10	.94
Maine	.06	.06	.10	.20	.19	.50	.43	.45	.11	.10	.12	.10	.97
Manitoba	.08	.08	.12	.25	.32	.55	.49	.51	.09	.08	.10	.10	.97
Maryland	.05	.06	.10	.20	.19	.50	.43	.45	.11	.10	.12	.10	.97
Massachusetts	.06	.06	.10	.20	.19	.50	.43	.45	.11	.10	.12	.10	.97
Mexico (A & C)	.18	.18	.22	.33	....	....	....	....	.19	.18	.20	.18	....
Mexico (B)	.07	.07	.11	....	....	....	....	....	.08	.07	.09	.07	....
Michigan	.06	.06	.10	.20	.22	.50	.46	.48	.11	.10	.12	.10	.94
Minnesota	.08	.08	.12	.25	.25	.50	.49	.51	.09	.08	.10	.08	.94
Minneapolis	.08	.08	.12	.25	....	.50	.49	.51	.09	.08	.10	.08	.94
Mississippi	.05	.05	.09	.20	.22	.50	.46	.48	.11	.10	.12	.10	.94
Missouri	.06	.06	.10	.25	.25	.55	.49	.51	.09	.08	.10	.08	.94
St. Louis	.06	.06	.10	.25	.25	.50	....	....	.09	.08	.10	.08	.94
Montana	.08	.08	.12	.25	.25	.55	.49	.51	.07	.06	.08	.08	.91
Nebraska	.08	.08	.12	.25	.25	.55	.49	.51	.09	.08	.10	.08	.91
Nevada	.10	.10	.14	.25	.28	.55	.50	.52	.07	.06	.08	.05	.91
N. B. & N. S	.06	.08	.12	.25	.26	.55	.56	.58	.11	.10	.12	.10	1.01
Newfoundland	.12	.14	.18	.25	....	.65	....	....	.17	.16	.18	.16	1.11
New Hampshire	.06	.06	.10	.20	.19	.50	.43	.45	.11	.10	.12	.10	.97
New Jersey	.06	.06	.10	.20	.19	.50	.43	.45	.11	.10	.12	.10	.97
New Mexico	.08	.08	.12	.25	.25	.55	.49	.51	.09	.08	.10	.08	.91
New York City	.06	.06	.10	.20	.16	.50	.40	.42	.11	.10	.12	.10	.97
New York	.06	.06	.10	.20	.19	.50	.43	.45	.11	.10	.12	.10	.97
North Carolina	.05	.05	.09	.20	.22	.50	.46	.48	.11	.10	.12	.10	.97
North Dakota	.08	.08	.12	.25	.25	.55	.49	.51	.09	.08	.10	.08	.91
Ohio	.06	.06	.10	.20	.22	.50	.46	.48	.11	.10	.12	.10	.94
Oklahoma	.08	.08	.12	.25	.25	.55	.49	.51	.09	.08	.10	.08	.94
Ontario	.08	.08	.12	.25	.26	.55	.56	.58	.11	.10	.12	.10	1.01
Oregon	.10	.10	.14	.25	.28	.55	.50	.52	.05	.04	.05	.05	.89
Philadelphia	.05	.06	.10	.20	.19	.50	.43	.45	.11	.10	.12	.10	.97
Pennsylvania	.06	.06	.10	.20	.19	.50	.43	.45	.11	.10	.12	.10	.97
Prince Edward Island	.08	.10	.14	.25	....	.55	....	....	.13	.12	.14	.12	1.07
Quebec	.08	.08	.12	.25	.26	.55	.56	.58	.11	.10	.12	.10	1.01
Rhode Island	.06	.06	.10	.20	.19	.50	.43	.45	.11	.10	.12	.10	.97
Saskatchewan	.10	.10	.14	.25	.32	....	.62	.64	.10	.09	.11	.10	....
South Carolina	.02	.05	.09	.20	.22	.50	.46	.48	.11	.10	.12	.10	.97
South Dakota	.08	.08	.12	.25	.25	.55	.49	.51	.09	.08	.10	.08	.91
Tennessee	.05	.05	.09	.20	.22	.50	.46	.48	.11	.10	.12	.10	.94
Texas	.06	.06	.10	.25	.25	.55	.45	.47	.09	.08	.10	.08	.94
Utah	.08	.08	.12	.25	.28	.55	.50	.52	.07	.06	.08	.06	.89
Vermont	.06	.06	.10	.20	.19	.50	.43	.45	.11	.10	.12	.10	.97
Virginia	.05	.05	.09	.20	.22	.50	.46	.48	.11	.10	.12	.10	.97
Washington	.10	.10	.14	.25	.28	.55	.50	.52	.04	.03	.06	.06	.89
West Virginia	.05	.06	.10	.20	.22	.50	.46	.48	.11	.10	.12	.10	.97
Wisconsin	.06	.06	.10	.20	.22	.50	.46	.48	.09	.08	.10	.08	.94
Wyoming	.08	.08	.12	.25	.25	.55	.49	.51	.09	.08	.10	.08	.91

NOTE.—Rates quoted for Key West, Tatoosh, and Cape Blanco include the charges for connecting lines between those stations and Western Union and Postal Telegraph Co.'s lines.

Rates quoted do NOT include radio charges.

For cable rates to other points use Western Union Tariff Book, pages 818 to 855, except that the cable rate from Key West, Fla., to Havana, Cuba, is 10 cents per word.

Charleston, St. Augustine, Pensacola, San Diego, and Tatoosh, in addition to Western Union connections, also have Postal connections; hence, on messages routed via these stations, the Postal Telegraph-Cable Co.'s Tariff Book, pages 543 to 605, may also be used for cable rates.

94. TABLE A1.—*Station rates and land-line rates from Marconi coast stations to various points.*

(Station rate subject to change.)

Between all offices below.	And coast stations at—																
	New York City, N. Y., Sea Gate, N. Y., Sagaponack, N. Y.	Point Judith, R. I., Boston, Mass., South Wellfleet, Mass.	Siasconset, Mass.	Cape May, N. J.	Philadelphia, Pa.	Baltimore, Md.	Virginia Beach, Va.	Hatteras, N. C.	Savannah, Ga.	Jacksonville, Fla., Tampa, Fla.	Mobile, Ala.	New Orleans, La.	Grand Island, La.	Galveston, Tex., Port Arthur, Tex.	East San Pedro, Cal., San Francisco, Cal., San Pedro, Cal.	Seattle, Wash., Astoria, Oreg., Marshfield, Oreg	Friday Harbor, Wash.
Station rate	$0.06	$0.06	$0.06	$0.06	$0.06	$0.06	$0.06	$0.06	$0.06	$0.06	$0.06	$0.06	$0.06	$0.06	$0.06	$0.06	$0.06
Alabama	.06	.06	.11	.06	.06	.06	.05	.06	.05	.05	.03	.05	.12	.05	.10	.10	.14
Alberta	.10	.10	.15	.10	.10	.10	.10	.11	.10	.10	.10	.10	.17	.10	.08	.06	.10
Arizona	.10	.10	.15	.10	.10	.10	.10	.11	.08	.10	.08	.08	.15	.08	.06	.08	.12
Arkansas	.06	.06	.11	.06	.06	.06	.06	.07	.05	.05	.05	.05	.12	.05	.10	.10	.14
British Columbia	.10	.10	.15	.10	.10	.10	.10	.11	.10	.10	.10	.10	.17	.10	.06	.05	.09
California	.10	.10	.15	.10	.10	.10	.10	.11	.10	.10	.10	.10	.17	.08	.04	.06	.10
Colorado	.08	.08	.13	.08	.08	.08	.08	.09	.08	.08	.08	.08	.15	.06	.08	.08	.12
Connecticut	.02	.02	.07	.04	.04	.04	.05	.06	.06	.06	.06	.06	.13	.08	.10	.10	.14
Delaware	.03	.04	.09	.04	.02	.02	.04	.05	.06	.06	.06	.06	.13	.08	.10	.10	.14
District of Columbia	.03	.04	.09	.04	.02	.02	.04	.05	.05	.06	.06	.05	.12	.08	.10	.10	.14
Florida (except Key West)	.06	.06	.11	.06	.06	.06	.05	.06	.05	.04	.05	.05	.12	.06	.10	.10	.14
Georgia	.06	.06	.11	.06	.06	.05	.05	.06	.02	.05	.05	.05	.12	.06	.10	.10	.14
Idaho	.10	.10	.15	.10	.10	.10	.10	.11	.10	.10	.10	.10	.17	.08	.06	.05	.09
Illinois	.05	.06	.11	.05	.05	.05	.05	.06	.06	.06	.06	..6	.13	.06	.08	.08	.12
Indiana	.05	.05	.10	.05	.05	.05	.05	.06	.06	.06	.06	.06	.13	.06	.10	.10	.14
Iowa	.06	.06	.11	.06	.06	.06	.06	.07	.06	.06	.06	.06	.13	.06	.08	.08	.12
Kansas	.06	.08	.13	.06	.06	.06	.06	.07	.06	.08	.06	.06	.13	.06	.08	.08	.12
Kentucky	.05	.06	.11	.05	.05	.05	.05	.06	.05	.05	.05	.05	.12	.06	.10	.10	.14
Louisiana	.06	.06	.11	.06	.06	.06	.06	.06	.05	.05	.05	.02	.09	.05	.10	.10	.14
Maine	.04	.03	.08	.05	.05	.05	.05	.06	.06	.06	.06	.06	.13	.08	.10	.10	.14
Manitoba	.08	.08	.13	.08	.08	.08	.08	.09	.08	.08	.08	.08	.15	.08	.10	.08	.12
Maryland	.03	.05	.10	.04	.03	.02	.04	.05	.05	.06	.06	.06	.13	.08	.10	.10	.14
Massachusetts	.03	.02	.07	.04	.04	.04	.05	.06	.06	.06	.06	.06	.13	.08	.10	.10	.14
Mexico (Classes A and C)	.18	.18	.23	.18	.18	.18	.18	.19	.18	.18	.18	.18	.25	.18	.18	.18	.22
Mexico (Class B)	.07	.07	.12	.07	.07	.07	.07	.08	.07	.07	.07	.07	.14	.07	.07	.07	.11
Michigan	.05	.05	.10	.05	.05	.05	.05	.06	.06	.06	.06	.06	.13	.08	.10	.10	.14
Minnesota	.06	.06	.11	.06	.06	.06	.06	.07	.08	.08	.08	.08	.15	.08	.06	.08	.12
Mississippi	.06	.06	.11	.06	.06	.06	.05	.06	.05	.05	.05	.04	.11	.05	.10	.10	.14

Missouri	.06	.06	.11	.06	.06	.06	.06	.07	.06	.06	.06	.06	.13	.06	.08	.08	.12
Montana	.08	.08	.13	.08	.08	.08	.08	.09	.08	.08	.08	.08	.15	.08	.08	.06	.10
Nebraska	.06	.08	.13	.06	.06	.06	.06	.07	.08	.08	.06	.08	.15	.06	.08	.08	.12
Nevada	.10	.10	.15	.10	.10	.10	.10	.11	.10	.10	.10	.10	.17	.08	.05	.06	.10
New Brunswick and Nova Scotia	.05	.05	.10	.05	.05	.05	.06	.07	.08	.08	.08	.08	.15	.08	.10	.10	.14
Newfoundland	.11	.11	.16	.11	.11	.11	.12	.13	.14	.14	.14	.14	.21	.14	.16	.16	.20
New Hampshire	.03	.03	.08	.04	.04	.04	.05	.06	.06	.06	.06	.06	.13	.08	.10	.10	.14
New Jersey	.02	.04	.09	.02	.02	.04	.05	.06	.06	.06	.06	.06	.13	.08	.10	.10	.14
New Mexico	.08	.08	.13	.08	.08	.08	.08	.09	.08	.08	.08	.08	.15	.06	.08	.08	.12
New York City	.02	.03	.08	.02	.02	.03	.05	.06	.06	.06	.06	.06	.13	.08	.10	.10	.14
New York	.03	.04	.09	.04	.04	.04	.05	.06	.06	.06	.06	.06	.13	.08	.10	.10	.14
North Carolina	.05	.06	.11	.05	.05	.05	.05	.06	.05	.05	.05	.05	.12	.06	.10	.10	.14
North Dakota	.08	.08	.13	.08	.08	.08	.08	.09	.08	.08	.08	.08	.15	.08	.08	.08	.12
Ohio	.04	.05	.10	.04	.04	.04	.05	.06	.06	.06	.06	.06	.13	.06	.10	.10	.14
Oklahoma	.08	.08	.13	.08	.08	.08	.08	.09	.06	.08	.06	.05	.12	.06	.08	.08	.12
Ontario	.05	.05	.10	.05	.05	.05	.06	.07	.08	.08	.08	.08	.15	.08	.10	.10	.14
Oregon	.10	.10	.15	.10	.10	.10	.10	.11	.10	.10	.10	.10	.17	.08	.05	.05	.09
Philadelphia	.02	.04	.09	.02	.02	.02	.05	.06	.06	.06	.06	.06	.13	.08	.10	.10	.14
Pennsylvania	.03	.04	.09	.04	.03	.04	.05	.06	.06	.06	.06	.06	.13	.08	.10	.10	.14
Prince Edward Island	.07	.07	.12	.07	.07	.07	.08	.09	.10	.10	.10	.10	.17	.10	.12	.12	.16
Quebec	.05	.05	.10	.05	.05	.05	.06	.07	.08	.08	.08	.08	.15	.08	.10	.10	.14
Rhode Island	.03	.02	.07	.04	.04	.04	.05	.06	.06	.06	.06	.06	.13	.08	.10	.10	.14
Saskatchewan	.10	.10	.15	.10	.10	.10	.10	.11	.10	.10	.10	.10	.17	.10	.10	.09	.13
South Carolina	.06	.06	.11	.06	.05	.05	.05	.06	.05	.05	.05	.05	.12	.06	.10	.10	.14
South Dakota	.08	.08	.13	.08	.08	.08	.08	.09	.08	.08	.08	.08	.15	.08	.08	.08	.12
Tennessee	.05	.05	.11	.05	.05	.05	.05	.06	.05	.05	.05	.05	.12	.06	.10	.10	.14
Texas	.08	.08	.13	.08	.08	.08	.08	.09	.06	.06	.05	.05	.12	.03	.08	.08	.12
Utah	.08	.08	.13	.08	.08	.08	.08	.09	.08	.08	.08	.08	.15	.08	.06	.06	.10
Vermont	.03	.03	.08	.04	.04	.04	.05	.06	.06	.06	.06	.05	.13	.08	.10	.10	.14
Virginia	.04	.05	.10	.05	.05	.04	.02	.03	.05	.05	.05	.05	.12	.08	.10	.10	.14
Washington	.10	.10	.15	.10	.10	.10	.10	.11	.10	.10	.10	.10	.17	.08	.06	.03	.07
West Virginia	.04	.05	.10	.04	.04	.04	.04	.05	.05	.06	.06	.06	.13	.08	.10	.10	.14
Wisconsin	.06	.06	.11	.06	.06	.06	.06	.07	.06	.06	.06	.06	.13	.08	.08	.08	.12
Wyoming	.08	.08	.13	.08	.08	.08	.06	.09	.08	.08	.08	.08	.15	.08	.08	.08	.12

NOTE.—Rates quoted do NOT include ship charges.
For cable rates to other points use Western Union Tariff Book, pages 818 to 855, except that the cable rate from Key West, Fla., to Havana, Cuba, is 10 cents per word.
Postal Tariff Book, pages 543 to 605, may also be used for cable rates.

95. TABLE B.—*Cable rates to the principal countries of the world from United States naval radio stations in the United States.*

[Rates quoted do not include the ship charges, which must be added.]

To—	From—										
	Charleston.	St. Augustine.	Jupiter.	Pensacola.	Key West.	Tatoosh.	North Head.	Cape Blanco.	Eureka.	Point Arguello.	San Diego.
Station rate	$0.05	$0.05	$0.05	$0.05	$0.05	$0.05	$0.05	$0.05	$0.05	$0.05	$0.05
Arabia:											
Aden	.80	.83	.83	.80	.86	.87	.86	.88	.86	.86	.86
Perim	.80	.83	.83	.80	.86	.87	.86	.88	.88	.86	.86
Australia and New Zealand	.66	.66	.66	.66	.66	.59	.58	.60	.58	.58	.58
Austria	.38	.41	.41	.38	.44	.45	.44	.46	.44	.44	.44
Belgium	.31	.34	.34	.31	.37	.38	.37	.39	.37	.37	.37
China [1]	1.22	1.22	1.22	1.22	1.22	1.15	1.14	1.16	1.14	1.14	1.14
Denmark	.41	.44	.44	.41	.47	.48	.47	.49	.47	.47	.47
Egypt:											
Port Said	.56	.59	.59	.56	.62	.63	.62	.64	.62	.62	.62
Suez	.56	.59	.59	.56	.62	.63	.62	.64	.62	.62	.62
Cairo	.56	.59	.59	.56	.62	.63	.62	.64	.62	.62	.62
Canal stations	.56	.59	.59	.56	.62	.63	.62	.64	.62	.62	.62
England	.31	.34	.34	.31	.37	.38	.37	.39	.37	.37	.37
France	.31	.34	.34	.31	.37	.38	.37	.39	.37	.37	.37
Germany	.31	.34	.34	.31	.37	.38	.37	.39	.37	.37	.37
Gibraltar	.49	.52	.52	.49	.55	.56	.55	.57	.55	.55	.55
Greece	.42	.45	.45	.42	.48	.49	.48	.50	.48	.48	.48
Guam	.95	.95	.95	.95	.99	.90	.89	.91	.89	.89	.89
Holland	.31	.34	.34	.31	.37	.38	.37	.39	.37	.37	.37
Honolulu	.47	.47	.47	.47	.47	.40	.39	.41	.39	.39	.39
Hungary	.38	.41	.41	.38	.44	.45	.44	.46	.44	.44	.44
India	.80	.83	.83	.80	.86	.87	.86	.88	.86	.86	.86
Ireland	.31	.34	.34	.31	.37	.38	.37	.39	.37	.37	.37
Italy	.37	.40	.40	.37	.43	.44	.43	.45	.43	.43	.43
Japan	1.33	1.33	1.33	1.33	1.33	1.26	1.25	1.27	1.25	1.25	1.25
Madeira	.56	.59	.59	.56	.62	.63	.62	.64	.62	.62	.62
Norway	.41	.44	.44	.41	.47	.48	.47	.49	.47	.47	.47
Philippines:											
Manila	1.12	1.12	1.12	1.12	1.12	1.05	1.04	1.06	1.04	1.04	1.04
Iloilo	1.27	1.27	1.27	1.27	1.27	1.20	1.19	1.21	1.19	1.19	1.19
Bacolod	1.27	1.27	1.27	1.27	1.27	1.20	1.19	1.21	1.19	1.19	1.19
Cebu	1.27	1.27	1.27	1.27	1.27	1.20	1.19	1.21	1.19	1.19	1.19
Portugal	.48	.48	.48	.45	.51	.52	.51	.53	.51	.51	.51
Russia in Europe	.49	.52	.52	.49	.55	.56	.55	.57	.55	.55	.55
Scotland	.31	.34	.34	.31	.37	.38	.37	.39	.37	.37	.37
Spain:											
Barcelona	.44	.47	.47	.44	.50	.51	.50	.52	.50	.50	.50
Gerrona	.44	.47	.47	.44	.50	.51	.50	.52	.50	.50	.50
Loreda	.44	.47	.47	.44	.50	.51	.50	.52	.50	.50	.50
Tarrigona	.44	.47	.47	.44	.50	.51	.50	.52	.50	.50	.50
Other offices	.46	.49	.49	.46	.52	.53	.52	.54	.52	.52	.52
Sweden	.44	.47	.47	.44	.42	.51	.50	.52	.50	.50	.50
Switzerland	.36	.39	.39	.36	.42	.44	.43	.45	.43	.43	.43
Turkey in Europe	.42	.45	.45	.42	.48	.49	.48	.50	.48	.48	.48
Wales	.31	.34	.34	.31	.37	.38	.37	.39	.37	.37	.37

[1] For rate to Macao add 5 cents to China rate.
Cable count, with a ten-word minimum, shall be used in computing radio charges.
The ten-word minimum does not apply in computing cable charges.

NOTE.—Messages for Honolulu and for all other places in the island of Oahu are delivered free. Messages for Hawaiian Islands beyond Honolulu are accepted only at sender's risk. Messages for the islands of Hawaii, Maui, and Kawai may be forwarded beyond Honolulu by mail or by wireless telegraph. The charge for the wireless transmission is $1.50 for ten words or less, and 15 cents for each word over ten (address and signature to be counted and charged for), in addition to the rate to Honolulu. There is no charge for mailing. "Via Wireless" must be signaled in the checks of messages to be forwarded by wireless telegraph. Messages for other Hawaiian Islands can only be forwarded by mail from Honolulu. The name of the island must appear in address of every message going beyond Honolulu.

96. TABLE C.—*Cable rates to South America from United States naval radio stations in the United States.*

[Rates quoted do not include the ship charges, which must be added.]

To—	From—										
	Charleston.	St. Augustine.	Jupiter.	Pensacola.	Key West.	Tatoosh.	North Head.	Cape Blanco.	Eureka.	Point Arguello.	San Diego.
Station rate	$0.05	$0.05	$0.05	$0.05	$0.05	$0.05	$0.05	$0.05	$0.05	$0.05	$0.05
Argentina	.71	.74	.74	.74	.77	.78	.77	.79	.77	.77	.77
Bolivia	.71	.74	.74	.74	.77	.78	.77	.79	.77	.77	.77
Brazil:											
Alemquer											
Amatary											
Itacoatiara											
Manaos											
Obidos											
Parintins											
San Jose	1.45	1.45	1.45	1.45	1.45	1.46	1.45	1.47	1.45	1.45	1.45
Antonio Lemas											
Breves											
Cameta											
Chaves											
Curralinho											
Gurupa											
Macagao											
Macapa											
Monte Alegre											
Mosqueiro											
Pinhairo											
Prainha											
Santarem											
Soure	1.15	1.15	1.15	1.15	1.15	1.16	1.15	1.17	1.15	1.15	1.15
Para											
Rio de Janeiro											
Rio Grande du Sul											
Santos	.85	.85	.85	.85	.85	.86	.85	.87	.85	.85	.85
Other offices	.85	.85	.85	.85	.85	.86	.85	.87	.85	.85	.85
Pernambuco	.70	.70	.70	.70	.70	.71	.70	.72	.70	.70	.70
British Guiana	1.08	1.08	1.08	1.08	1.08	1.14	1.13	1.15	1.13	1.13	1.13
Chile	.71	.74	.74	.74	.74	.78	.77	.79	.77	.77	.77
Dutch Guiana	1.38	1.38	1.38	1.38	1.38	1.44	1.43	1.45	1.43	1.43	1.43
Equador	.71	.74	.74	.74	.77	.78	.77	.79	.77	.77	.77
French Guiana	1.38	1.38	1.38	1.38	1.38	1.44	1.43	1.45	1.43	1.43	1.43
Paraguay	.71	.74	.74	.74	.77	.78	.78	.80	.78	.78	.78
Peru:											
Iquitos											
Masisea											
Orellana											
Requena	1.21	1.24	1.24	1.24	1.27	1.28	1.28	1.30	1.28	1.28	1.28
Other offices	.71	.74	.74	.74	.77	.78	.78	.80	.78	.78	.78
Republic of Panama	.46	.49	.49	.49	.49	.51	.51	.53	.51	.51	.51
United States of Colombia:											
Buenaventura	.71	.74	.74	.74	.77	.78	.77	.79	.77	.77	.77
Other offices	.76	.79	.79	.79	.82	.83	.82	.84	.82	.82	.82
Uruguay	.71	.74	.74	.74	.77	.78	.77	.79	.77	.77	.77
Venezuela	1.00	1.00	1.00	1.00	1.00	1.06	1.05	1.07	1.05	1.05	1.05

NOTE 1.—Messages for all offices in Costa Rica, Guatemala, Honduras, Nicaragua, and Salvador, South America, are accepted only at sender's risk, except to San Jose, in Guatemala; San Juan del Sur, in Nicaragua; and La Libertad, in Salvador.

NOTE 2.—Republic of Panama, United States of Colombia, Ecuador, Peru, and Venezuela refuse to investigate complaints concerning the transmission or delivery of telegrams passing over their lines, or to refund the charges paid therefor, under any circumstances whatever. Messages for stations on such lines can, therefore, be accepted only at sender's risk. The foregoing notice does not apply to telegrams destined for Colon and Panama, in Republic of Panama; Buenaventura, in the United States of Colombia; Guayaquil and St. Elena, in Ecuador; Callao, Lima, Mollendo, and Payta, in Peru; or Caracas and La Guayra, in Venezuela.

NOTE 3.—Messages via "New York-Colon" to Brazil are forwarded by land lines beyond Buenos Ayres; if desired, they will be forwarded by cables beyond that place at rate of 94 cents per word more than rate to Buenos Ayres.

NOTE 4.—Messages to be mailed to places beyond the telegraph lines in Ecuador will hereafter be routed via Guayaquil, and mailed therefrom. Messages whose addresses show other mailing routes should be refused.

29732°—14——3

97. TABLE D.—*Cable rates to the West Indies from United States naval radio stations in the United States.*

[Rates quoted do not include the ship charges, which must be added.]

To—	From—										
	Charleston.	St. Augustine.	Jupiter.	Pensacola.	Key West.	North Head.	Tatoosh.	Cape Blanco.	Eureka.	Point Arguello.	San Diego.
Station rate	$0.05	$0.05	$0.05	$0.05	$0.05	$0.05	$0.05	$0.05	$0.05	$0.05	$0.05
Antigua	.81	.81	.81	.81	.81	.86	.87	.88	.86	.86	.86
Barbados	.91	.91	.91	.91	.91	.96	.97	.98	.96	.96	.96
Bahamas	.35	.30	.25	.30	.35	.45	.46	.47	.45	.45	.45
Bermuda	.48	.51	.51	.48	.54	.54	.55	.56	.54	.54	.54
British Guiana	1.08	1.08	1.08	1.08	1.08	1.13	1.14	1.15	1.13	1.13	1.13
Cuba:											
Habana	.15	.15	.15	.15	.10	.20	.21	.22	.20	.20	.20
Other offices	.20	.20	.20	.20	.20	.25	.26	.27	.25	.25	.25
Curacao	1.38	1.38	1.38	1.38	1.38	1.43	1.44	1.45	1.43	1.43	1.43
Dominica	.77	.77	.77	.77	.77	.82	.83	.84	.82	.82	.82
Dutch Guiana	1.38	1.38	1.38	1.38	1.38	1.43	1.44	1.45	1.43	1.43	1.43
French Guiana	1.38	1.38	1.38	1.38	1.38	1.43	1.44	1.45	1.43	1.43	1.43
Grenada	.89	.89	.89	.89	.89	.94	.95	.96	.94	.94	.94
Guadaloupe	1.00	1.00	1.00	1.00	1.00	1.05	1.06	1.07	1.05	1.05	1.05
Hayti:											
Cape Haitien	.80	.80	.80	.80	.80	.85	.86	.87	.85	.85	.85
Mole St. Nicholas	.80	.80	.80	.80	.80	.85	.86	.87	.85	.85	.85
Port au Prince	.80	.80	.80	.80	.80	.85	.86	.87	.85	.85	.85
Other offices	1.55	1.55	1.55	1.55	1.55	1.60	1.61	1.62	1.60	1.60	1.60
Jamaica	.48	.48	.48	.48	.48	.53	.54	.55	.53	.53	.53
Les Saintes	1.00	1.00	1.00	1.00	1.00	1.05	1.06	1.07	1.05	1.05	1.05
Marie Galante	1.00	1.00	1.00	1.00	1.00	1.05	1.06	1.07	1.05	1.05	1.05
Martinique	1.00	1.00	1.00	1.00	1.00	1.05	1.06	1.07	1.05	1.05	1.05
Porto Rico	.50	.50	.50	.50	.50	.55	.56	.57	.55	.55	.55
St. Kitts	.89	.89	.89	.89	.89	.94	.95	.96	.94	.94	.94
St. Croix [1]	1.02	1.02	1.02	1.02	1.02	1.07	1.08	1.09	1.07	1.07	1.07
St. Lucia	.85	.85	.85	.85	.85	.90	.91	.92	.90	.90	.90
St. Thomas	.96	.96	.96	.96	.96	1.01	1.02	1.03	1.01	1.01	1.01
St. Vincent	.86	.86	.86	.86	.86	.91	.92	.93	.91	.91	.91
Santo Domingo	1.32	1.32	1.32	1.32	1.32	1.37	1.38	1.39	1.37	1.37	1.37
Trinidad	.98	.98	.98	.98	.98	1.03	1.04	1.05	1.03	1.03	1.03

[1] There is a local Government line charge between Christiansted and Frederiksted, St. Croix, i. e., 20 cents per message of 20 words or less, cable count, plus 10 cents for each additional 10 words or less, which amount should be added to the rates given above.

Cable count, with a 10-word minimum, shall be used in computing radio charges.

The 10-word minimum does not apply in computing cable charges.

98. TABLE E.—*Cable rates to Mexico, Central and South America from United States naval radio stations at San Juan, P. R., Guantanamo Bay, Cuba, and Colon, C. Z.*

[Rates quoted do not include the ship and station charges, which must be added.]

To—	From—				
	Guantanamo.		San Juan.	Colon.	
	C. F. d. C. T.	C. & S. A. T. C.	W. I. & P. T. C.	W. I. & P. T. C.	C. & S. A. T. C.
Argentina:					
Buenos Aires, Rosario, Mendoza, and Villa Mercedes [1]	$0.85	$0.79	$1.34	....	$0.55
Other offices	.85	.87	1.42	....	.63
Bolivia	.85	.74	1.29	....	.50
Brazil:					
Except Amazon River stations	1.07	1.11	1.50	....	.87
Amazon River, first zone	1.32	1.41	1.75	....	1.17
Amazon River, second zone	1.62	1.71	2.05	....	1.47
British Guiana:					
Georgetown	1.49	1.28	1.27	$1.43	1.94
Other offices	1.49	1.28	1.29	1.45	1.94
Chile:					
Iqueque, Antofagasta, Valparaiso, Santiago, Quillota, and Los Andes	.85	.54	1.09	....	.30
Other offices	.85	.57	1.12	....	.33
Costa Rica	.75	.44	.99	....	.20
Dutch Guiana	1.22	1.58	.91	1.48	1.88
Ecuador:					
Santa Elena and Esmeralda	.85	.64	1.19	....	.40
Guayaquil	.85	.69	1.24	....	.45
Other offices	.85	.74	1.29	....	.50
French Guiana:					
Cayenne	1.22	1.58	1.31	1.67	1.88
Other offices	1.26	1.58	1.31	1.67	1.88
Guatemala:					
San Jose de Guatemala	.66	.44	.99	....	.20
Other offices	.71	.49	1.04	....	.25
Honduras	.75	.49	1.04	....	.25
Mexico:					
Mexico City, Veracruz, Coatzacoalcos, and Salina Cruz	.38	.54	[2] .93	....	.30
Other offices (except radio stations)	.41	.57	.96	....	.33
Radio stations	....	.62	([3])	....	.38
Nicaragua:					
San Juan del Sur	.70	.39	.94	....	.15
Other offices	.75	.44	.99	....	.20
Paraguay	....	.87	1.42	....	.63
Peru:					
Paita, Callao, and Lima	.85	.64	1.19	....	.40
Other offices (except radio stations and special 56-cent-rate stations)	....	.69	1.24	....	.45
Radio stations	....	.90	....	....	.90
Salvador:					
La Libertad	.70	.44	.99	....	.20
Other offices	.75	.49	1.04	....	.25
United States of Colombia:					
Buenaventura	.85	.54	1.09	....	.30
Other offices	.90	.64	1.19	....	.40
Uruguay:					
Montevideo	.85	.84	1.39	....	.60
Other offices	.85	.91	1.46	....	.67
Venezuela	1.10	1.20	1.33	1.35	1.35

[1] Villa Mercedes is rated "other offices" by W. I. & P. T. Co., hence rate from San Juan would be $1.42. Cable count with a minimum of 10 words shall be used in computing radio charges.
The 10-word minimum does not apply in computing cable charges.

[2] As Coatzacoalcos and Salina Cruz are considered "other offices" by the W. I. & P. T. Co., the rate from San Juan to those places is $0.96, the $0.93 rate appearing in the table applying only to Mexico City and Veracruz.

[3] The rate from San Juan to Tampico, Mexico, is $1.01. The rate from San Juan to the Island of Trinidad is $0.86.

99. TABLE F.—*Cable rates to principal countries of the world and West Indian Islands from United States naval radio stations at Guantanamo Bay, Cuba, San Juan, P. R., and Colon, C. Z.*

[Rates quoted do not include the ship and station charges, which must be added.]

To—	From—				
	Guantanamo.		San Juan.	Colon.	
	C. F. d. C. T.	C. & S. A. T. C.	W. I. & P. T. C.	W. I. & P. T. C.	C. & S. A. T. C.
Antigua	$0.86	$1.01	$0.33	$0.95	$1.31
Austria	.52	.52	1.07	.82	.82
Bahamas	.45	.55			.85
Barbados	.96	1.11	.76	1.17	1.41
Belgium	.45	.45	1.00	.75	.75
Bermuda	.62	.02			.92
China		1.42			1.72
Colon and Canal Zone	.55	.30	.79		
Cuba:					
Habana		.35	.45	.35	.40
Santiago		.40	.60	.45	.45
Other offices		.40	.45	.35	.45
Canaries	.72	.72	1.27		1.02
Curaçao	1.08	1.58	1.51	1.53	1.53
Denmark	.55	.55	1.10	.85	.85
Dominica	.82	.97	.47	1.03	1.27
England	.45	.45	1.00	.75	.75
France	.45	.45	1.00	.75	.75
Germany	.45	.45	1.00	.75	.75
Gibraltar	.63	.63	1.18		.93
Greece		.56	1.11	.86	.86
Grenada	.94	1.09	.74	1.16	1.39
Guadeloupe:					
Basse-Terre	.82	1.20	.41	1.00	1.50
Point a Pitre	.82	1.20	.43	1.00	1.50
Haiti:					
Mole St. Nicholas	.50	1.00	1.10	.95	.70
Port au Prince and Cape Haitien	.60	1.00	1.20	1.05	.70
Other offices	1.10	1.50	1.70	1.55	1.45
Holland	.45	.45	1.00	.75	.75
Honolulu		.67			.97
Hungary	.52	.52	1.07	.82	.82
India		.94			1.24
Ireland	.45	.45	1.00	.75	.75
Italy	.51	.51	1.06	.81	.81
Jamaica:					
Kingston and Holland Bay	.38	.68	.84	.50	.73
Other offices	.38	.68	.86	.52	.77
Japan		1.53			1.83
Madeira		.70			1.00
Martinique	.82	1.20	.52	1.05	1.50
Norway	.55	.55	1.10	.85	.85
Panama Republic	.55	.33	.83		
Philippine Islands:					
Manila		1.32			1.62
Porto Rico:					
San Juan and Ponce	.80	.70		.79	1.25
Other offices	.80	.70		.83	1.25
Portugal		.59	1.14	.89	.89
Russia in Europe		.63			.93
San Domingo or Santo Domingo	1.00	1.52	1.33	1.45	1.45
St. Croix	1.07	1.22	.14	.86	1.52
St. Kitts	.94	1.09	.27	.93	1.39
St. Lucia	.90	1.05	.58	1.08	1.35
St. Thomas	1.01	1.16	.09	.93	1.46
St. Vincent	.91	1.06	.65	1.11	1.36
Scotland	.45	.45	1.00	.75	.75
Spain:					
Barcelona	.58	.58	1.13	.88	.88
Other offices	.58	.60	1.15	.90	.90
Sweden		.58			.88
Switzerland	.50	.50	1.05	.80	.80
Turkey in Europe		.56			.86
Wales	.45	.45	1.00	.75	.75

Cable count, with a minimum of 10 words, shall be used in computing radio charges.
The 10-word minimum does not apply in computing cable charges.

100. TABLE G.—*Rates of miscellaneous companies.*

Rates of Cuban Telegraph Co. from Guantanamo Bay to Any Point in Cuba.

Four cents per word, cable count, with a 10-word minimum.

Rates of Insular Telegraph Co., Island of Porto Rico.

For all points in the island, except Vieques, 2 cents per word, cable count, with a 10-word minimum.

For Vieques, 4 cents per word, cable count, with a 10-word minimum.

A special delivery charge of 10 cents per message is made on messages destined to Pta de Tierra, that is, stop 1 to 10.

Messages destined to Guayanilla, Penuelas, and Lajas have an extra charge of 25 cents per message on account of a telephone charge.

Rates of the Panama Railroad Telegraph Co.

Two cents per word, cable count, with a 10-word minimum.

Rates of Panamanian Government Telegraph Lines.

One cent per word, cable count, with a 10-word minimum.

101. TABLE H.—*Word rates for commercial messages sent through naval radio stations in Alaska.*

SIGNAL CORPS RATES FROM ALASKAN NAVAL RADIO STATIONS TO POINTS IN ALASKA.

To—	From—					
	Pribilofs, Dutch Harbor, Unalga.		Kodiak.		Cordova.	Sitka.
	Via Cordova.	Via Nome. (Army.)	Via Cordova.	Via Sitka.		
Beaver Dam	$0.08	....	$0.08	....	$0.08	$0.21
Birches	....	$0.17	.20	....	.20	.26
Boundary	.15	....	.15	....	.15	.22
Chena	.15	....	.15	....	.15	.26
Circle	.15	....	.15	....	.15	.20
Copper Center	.09	....	.09	....	.09	.21
Cordova	.02	....	.02	....	.02	.16
Delta	.15	....	.15	....	.15	.26
Donnely	.14	....	.14	....	.14	.26
Douglas	.22	....	....	$0.09	.22	.09
Eureka	.17	....	.17	....	.17	.26
Fairbanks	.15	....	.15	....	.15	.26
Fort Davis	....	.07	.29	....	.29	.30
Fort Egbert	.15	....	.15	....	.15	.20
Fort Gibbon	....	.18	.18	....	.18	.26
Fort Liscum	.08	....	.08	....	.08	.16
Golsova	....	.13	.23	....	.23	.26
Gulkana	.09	....	.09	....	.09	.21
Haines	.21	....	....	.10	.21	.10
Hadley	.21	....	....	.10	.21	.10
Hogan	.11	....	.11	....	.11	.23
Hot Springs	.17	....	.17	....	.17	.25
Juneau	.21	....	....	.08	.21	.08
Kaltag	....	.14	.22	....	.22	.26
Ketchikan	.21	....	....	.10	.21	.10
Kokrines	....	.17	.20	....	.20	.26
Kotlik	....	.11	.29	....	.29	.30
Koyukuk	....	.14	.22	....	.22	.26
Louden	....	.15	.21	....	.21	.26
McCallum	.13	....	.13	....	.13	.25
McCarty	.15	....	.15	....	.15	.26

TABLE H.—*Word rates for commercial messages sent through naval radio stations in Alaska*—Continued.

SIGNAL CORPS RATES FROM ALASKAN NAVAL RADIO STATIONS TO POINTS IN ALASKA—Continued.

To—	From—					
	Pribilofs, Dutch Harbor, Unalga.		Kodiak.		Cordova.	Sitka.
	Via Cordova.	Via Nome. (Army.)	Via Cordova.	Via Sitka.		
Melozi		$0.17	$0.20		$0.20	$0.26
Minto	$0.15		.15		.15	.26
Nenana	.15		.15		.15	.26
Nome		.05	.29		.29	.30
Nulato		.14	.22		.22	.26
Old Woman		.14	.22		.22	.26
Paxson	.12		.12		.12	.24
Petersburg	.22			$0.12	.22	.12
Rampart		.18	.20		.20	.26
Richardson	.15		.15		.15	.26
St. Michael		.11	.23		.23	.26
Salcha	.15		.15		.15	.26
Seward	.11		.11		.11	.21
Sitka	.16			.02	.16	.02
Skagway	.21			.11	.21	.11
Teikhell	.08		.08		.08	.21
Thompsons Pass	.08		.08		.08	.21
Tolovana	.17		.17		.17	.26
Tonsina	.08		.08		.08	.21
Unalakleet		.13	.23		.23	.26
Valdez	.06		.06		.06	.16
Wortmans	.08		.08		.08	.21
Wrangell	.18			.08	.18	.08

NOTE.—The above table includes the Nome (Army) Radio Station charge of 5 cents per word on messages routed via Nome. On messages routed via Sitka or Cordova the 2 cents per word cable charge is included to cover the cable charge between Sitka and Cordova radio stations and the Signal Corps stations at Sitka and Cordova.

WESTERN UNION RATES FROM NORTH HEAD TO POINTS IN UNITED STATES.

	North Head.		North Head.
Alabama	$0.10	New Brunswick and Nova Scotia	$0.10
Arizona	.08	New Hampshire	.10
Arkansas	.10	New Jersey	.10
British Columbia	.05	New Mexico	.08
California [1]	.06	New York City	.10
Colorado	.08	New York State	.10
Connecticut	.10	North Carolina	.10
Delaware	.10	North Dakota	.08
District of Columbia	.10	Ohio	.10
Florida (except Key West)	.10	Oklahoma	.08
Georgia	.10	Ontario	.10
Idaho	.05	Oregon	.05
Illinois	.08	Philadelphia	.10
Indiana	.10	Pennsylvania	.10
Iowa	.08	Prince Edward Island	.12
Kansas	.08	Quebec	.10
Kentucky	.10	Rhode Island	.10
Louisiana	.10	South Carolina	.10
Maine	.10	South Dakota	.08
Manitoba	.08	Tennessee	.10
Maryland	.10	Texas	.08
Massachusetts	.10	Utah	.06
Michigan	.10	Vermont	.10
Minnesota	.08	Virginia	.10
Mississippi	.10	Washington	.03
Missouri	.08	West Virginia	.10
Montana	.06	Wisconsin	.08
Nebraska	.08	Wyoming	.08
Nevada	.06		

[1] Eureka to any point in California is 4 cents per word.

Messages from Ships at Sea to Points in the United States.

Messages from ships at sea addressed to points in the United States will be charged as follows:

Via St. Paul (Pribilofs), Dutch Harbor, Unalga, and Kodiak to all points in the United States, except California, via North Head, Wash., radio station, 25 cents per word, plus the Western Union word rate from North Head, as shown above, to destination.

Via St. Paul (Pribilofs), Dutch Harbor, Unalga, and Kodiak to points in California, via Eureka radio station, 30 cents per word, plus the Western Union word rate from Eureka, as shown above, to destination.

Via Cordova and Sitka to all points in the United States, except California, via North Head radio station, 26 and 16 cents, respectively, plus the Western Union word rate from North Head, as shown above, to destination.

Via Cordova and Sitka to all points in California, via Eureka radio station, 31 and 21 cents, respectively, plus the Western Union word rate from Eureka, as shown above, to destination.

A message intended for any point in the United States, except California, will be sent by radio to North Head through any station able to handle the work, relayed if necessary. A message intended for California will be sent similarly by radio to Eureka.

Messages Filed at Naval Radio Stations in Alaska or Delivered to Said Stations by Army Signal Corps Lines for Points in United States.

Use above rate less 5 cents per word for Navy charge plus Western Union rate to destination.

Messages Filed at Naval Radio Stations in Alaska for any Point in Alaska.

Five cents per word for radio rate plus Signal Corps rate to destination.

Messages from Ships in Alaskan Waters to Points in the United States.

Five cents per word for radio charge plus Signal Corps rate from Cordova, Sitka, or Nome to destination, as per table above.

(See Table I for Army radio rates.)

Messages Filed at or Transferred to an Alaskan Naval Radio Station Addressed to Another Alaskan Naval Radio Station.

Charges are 5 cents per word, except:

Between Cordova naval radio station and Sitka naval radio station, where the charge will be the Army cable charge of 14 cents per word.

General Notes Applicable to Above Tables.

The above rates must be used exclusively, and messages must be routed, as per table, for Alaskan points.

EXAMPLE No. 1.

Message from North Head to Birches, Fort Davis, Fort Gibbon, Golsova, etc., must be routed via Nome; likewise a message from sea via Dutch Harbor to these points is routed via Nome.

EXAMPLE No. 2.

Message from North Head to Douglas, Haines, Juneau, etc., route via Sitka; or if from sea, via Kodiak, route via Sitka to above points.

EXAMPLE No. 3.

Message from sea via Pribilofs to Beaver Dam, Boundary, Chena, etc., route via Cordova.

The rate via Nome has the Nome Signal Corps radio charge of 5 cents included.

On messages addressed to towns of Cordova or Sitka there is a 2 cents per word Signal Corps charge, as per table. As the radio stations at those places are connected with the towns above mentioned by cable, this charge is, however, included in the Signal Corps table published herewith.

All charges are for a 10-word minimum message.

Cordova-Katalla Telephone Rate.

The rate between Cordova and Katalla is $1.25 for 10 words and 8 cents for each additional word.

102. TABLE I.—*Word rates for commercial messages sent through Army radio stations in Alaska.*

SIGNAL-CORPS RATES FROM ALASKAN ARMY RADIO STATIONS TO POINTS IN ALASKA AND TO SEATTLE, WASH.

To—	United States Army radio stations.				
	Via Nome.	Via St. Michael.	Via Kotlik.	Via Petersburg.	Via Wrangell.
Beaver Dam [1]	$0.28	$0.22	$0.28	$0.30	$0.26
Birches	.17	.12	.17	.35	.31
Boundary [1]	.27	.21	.27	.31	.27
Chena [1]	.22	.15	.22	.35	.31
Circle [1]	.25	.20	.25	.29	.25
Copper Center [1]	.28	.21	.28	.30	.26
Cordova [1]	.32	.26	.32	.25	.26
Delta [1]	.24	.17	.24	.35	.31
Donnely [1]	.26	.19	.26	.35	.31
Douglas [1]	.39	.34	.39	.14	.10
Eureka [1]	.20	.14	.20	.35	.31
Fairbanks [1]	.22	.15	.22	.35	.31
Fort Davis	.07	.11	.11	.39	.35
Fort Egbert [1]	.25	.20	.25	.29	.25
Fort Gibbon	.18	.14	.18	.35	.31
Fort Liscum [1]	.28	.22	.28	.25	.21
Golsova	.13	.07	.13	.35	.31
Gulkana [1]	.28	.21	.28	.30	.26
Hadley	.38	.34	.38	.13	.09
Haines [1]	.38	.33	.38	.17	.13
Hogan [1]	.29	.22	.29	.32	.28
Hot Springs [1]	.20	.14	.20	.34	.30
Juneau [1]	.38	.33	.38	.13	.09
Kaltag	.14	.08	.14	.35	.31
Ketchikan [1]	.38	.34	.38	.13	.09

[1] For an alternative or lower rate to these points, when transmitted *via* naval radio stations, see Table II. For rates to other points in Alaska and to points in British Columbia consult Signal Corps Tariff Book, 1914. The above includes the Army radio shore station charge of 5 cents per word.

TABLE I.—*Word rates for commercial messages sent through Army radio stations in Alaska*—Continued.

SIGNAL-CORPS RATES FROM ALASKAN RADIO STATIONS TO POINTS IN ALASKA AND TO SEATTLE, WASH.—Continued.

To—	United States Army radio stations.				
	Via Nome.	Via St. Michael.	Via Kotlik.	Via Petersburg.	Via Wrangell.
Kokrines	$0.17	$0.11	$0.17	$0.35	$0.31
Kotlik	.11	.11	.05	.39	.35
Koyukuk	.14	.08	.14	.35	.31
Louden	.15	.09	.15	35	.31
McCallum [1]	.27	.20	27	.34	.30
McCarty [1]	.24	.17	.24	.35	.31
Melozi	.17	.11	.17	.35	.31
Minto [1]	.22	.16	.22	.35	.31
Nenana [1]	.22	.16	.22	.35	.31
Nome	.05	.11	.11	.39	.35
Nulato	.14	.08	.14	.35	.31
Old Woman	.14	.08	.14	.35	.31
Paxson [1]	.28	.21	.28	.33	.29
Petersburg [1]	.39	.35	.39	.05	.09
Rampart	.18	.14	.18	.35	.31
Richardson [1]	.24	.17	.24	.35	.31
St. Michael	.11	.05	.11	.35	.31
Salcha [1]	.22	.16	.22	.35	.31
Seattle [1]	.43	.38	.43	.25	.21
Seward [1]	.33	.27	.33	.30	.26
Sitka [1]	.33	.29	.33	.15	.11
Skagway [1]	.38	.33	.38	.17	.13
Teikhell [1]	.28	.20	.28	.30	.26
Thompson's Pass	.28	.22	.28	.30	.26
Tolovana [1]	.20	.14	.20	.35	.31
Tonsina [1]	.28	.22	.28	.30	.26
Unalakleet	.13	.07	.13	.35	.31
Valdez [1]	.28	.22	.28	.25	.21
Wortmans [1]	.28	.22	.28	.30	.26
Wrangell [1]	.35	.31	.35	.09	.05

[1] For an alternative or lower rate to these points, when transmitted *via* naval radio stations, see Table H. For rates to other points in Alaska and to points in British Columbia consult Signal Corps Tariff Book, 1914. The above includes the Army radio shore station charge of 5 cents per word.

WESTERN UNION RATES FROM SEATTLE TO POINTS IN UNITED STATES.

	Seattle.		Seattle.
Alabama	$0.10	New Brunswick and Nova Scotia	$0.10
Arizona	.08	New Hampshire	.10
Arkansas	.10	New Jersey	.10
British Columbia	.05	New Mexico	.08
California	.06	New York City	.10
Colorado	.08	New York State	.10
Connecticut	.10	North Carolina	.10
Delaware	.10	North Dakota	.08
District of Columbia	.10	Ohio	.10
Florida (except Key West)	.10	Oklahoma	.08
Georgia	.10	Ontario	.10
Idaho	.05	Oregon	.05
Illinois	.08	Philadelphia	.10
Indiana	.10	Pennsylvania	.10
Iowa	.08	Prince Edward Island	.12
Kansas	.08	Quebec	.10
Kentucky	.10	Rhode Island	.10
Louisiana	.10	South Carolina	.10
Maine	.10	South Dakota	.08
Manitoba	.08	Tennessee	.10
Maryland	.10	Texas	.08
Massachusetts	.10	Utah	.06
Michigan	.10	Vermont	.10
Minnesota	.08	Virginia	.10
Mississippi	.10	Washington	.03
Missouri	.08	West Virginia	.10
Montana	.06	Wisconsin	.08
Nebraska	.08	Wyoming	.08
Nevada	.06		

Messages from Ships at Sea to Points in the United States via Army Radio Stations.

Messages from ships at sea, *via* Army radio stations at Nome, St. Michael, or Kotlik, routed over Signal Corps land lines to Seattle, Wash., use the rate to Seattle, as per the above table, plus the Western Union rate from Seattle to destination.

If transmitted *via* the Army radio stations at Petersburg or Wran gell use rate of 25 and 21 cents respectively plus the Western Union word rate from Seattle to destination. (See example (*e*) par. 69.)

Messages from Ships at Sea to Points in the United States via Naval Radio Stations at Cordova or Sitka.

Messages from ships at sea, *via* the naval radio stations at Cordova or Sitka, may be transmitted to destination by several routes, at the option of the sender, viz:

(*a*) To all points in the United States, except California, through the North Head naval radio station, 26 and 16 cents, respectively, plus the Western Union rate from North Head (see Table H) to destination.

(*b*) To all points in California, through the Eureka naval radio station, 31 and 21 cents, respectively, plus the Western Union rate from Eureka (see Table H) to destination.

(*c*) To all points in the United States, including California, routed over Signal Corps lines to Seattle, 26 and 16 cents, respectively, plus the Western Union word rate from Seattle to destination. (See table above.)

(*d*) For rates to the United States through *other* naval radio stations. (See Table H.)

Messages from Points in the United States to Ships in Alaskan Waters via Army Radio Stations.

Use Western Union word rate from office of origin to Seattle, plus the Signal Corps word rate to the Army radio station, as per the above table (and route accordingly), plus the ship charge if not addressed to an Army transport.

Messages from Points in the United States to Ships in Alaskan Waters via Signal Corps and Naval Radio Stations.

Use Western Union word rate from office of origin to Seattle, plus 26 cents per word if transmitted through Cordova and 16 cents per word if transmitted through Sitka, plus naval radio charge of 5 cents per word. This does not include the ship charge, which must be added.

Messages from Points in Alaska to Ships at Sea via Army Radio Stations.

Use local rate from office of origin to the radio station, plus 5 cents per word for shore radio charge. This does not include the ship charge, which must be added if not addressed to an Army transport.

Messages from Points in Alaska to Ships at Sea via Naval Radio Stations at Cordova or Sitka.

Use the local rate from office of origin to Cordova or Sitka, as the case may be (and route accordingly), plus 2 cents per word for connecting cable charge, all of which is "this line." This does not include the naval radio shore rate of 5 cents per word, nor the ship charge, which must be added.

FOREIGN CABLE CHARGES.

Messages from Ships at Sea to Foreign Points via Army Radio Stations.

103. For this class of messages there is a straight cable rate of 30 cents per word on the exact number of words in the message, cable count, from any Army radio station in Alaska to Seattle, to which should be added the cable rate from Seattle to destination, as shown on pages 818 to 855 Western Union Tariff Book (or Postal Telegraph-Cable Co.'s Tariff Book, pages 543 to 605). The word rate, computed from the Army radio station to destination, is based on the exact number of words in the message. The 10-word minimum in messages of this class will apply only to the radio charge, which must be added.

104. TABLE K.—*Rates for commercial messages sent through the Army radio station at Corregidor, P. I.*

INSULAR GOVERNMENT RATES FROM MANILA TO POINTS IN THE PHILIPPINE ISLANDS.

To any telegraph office in the Province of—	For 10 words or less in the body.	To any telegraph office in the Province of—	For 10 words or less in the body.
Albay	$0.50	Lanao district, except Malabang	$0.90
Ambos Camarines	.40	Malabang:	
Antique	.70	Lanao district	1.00
Baatan	.20	Sulu district	1.30
Batangas	.20	Zamboanga district	1.20
Bohol	.80	Mountain	.40
Bulacan	.20	Nueva Ecija	.30
Cagayan	.50	Nueva Viscaya	.40
Capiz, except Rombion subprovince	.60	Occidental Negros	.80
Rombion subprovince	.50	Oriental Negros	.80
Cavite	.20	Palavan, except Cuyo	.90
Cebu	.80	Cuyo, Palavan Province	.80
Ilocos Norte	.50	Pampanga	.20
Ilocos Sur	.40	Pangasinan	.30
Iloilo	.70	Rizal	.20
Isabela	.40	Samar	.70
Laguna	.20	Sorgoson, except Masbate	.50
La Union	.40	Masbate, subprovince	.60
Leyte	.80	Surigao	.80
Manila	.20	Tarlac	.30
Mindoro, except San Jose	.40	Tabayas, except Marinduque	.30
San Jose, Mindoro Province	.60	Marinduque subprovince	.40
Misamis	.90	Zambales	.30
Moro:			
Cotabato district	1.00		
Davao district	1.30		
Dapitan district	....		

Does not include radio charge which must be added.

Additional words in the body: One-twentieth of the rate shown above for 10 words. For example, when the rate on 10 words is $1, each additional word is 5 cents. The rates quoted are in United States currency. The Philippine *peso* (₱1) may be accepted at 50 cents.

NOTE.—In computing rates to the above points from ships at sea it will be necessary to make two counts, i. e., *the radio count*, which will include the address and signature; and the land-line count, which will be computed on a 10-word basis, exclusive of the address and signature.

Rates via Insular Government Radio Stations.

The secretary, commerce and police, bureau of posts, Manila, P. I., has approved a coastal or shore station rate of 60 cents for 10 words or less, not counting the address or signature, and of 3 cents for each word in excess of 10 words in the body of the message, on all messages received from wireless shipboard stations. To this charge is to be added the regular zone rate to destination in the Philippine Islands. Operators on Army transports should ascertain by service message the zone rate beyond the shore station. *This does not include the shipboard radio charges which must be added.* (AGO 2126827.)

Via Commercial Cable.

Messages for the towns of Iloilo, Bacolod, and Cebu may also be transmitted, via commercial cable, direct from Manila at a rate of 15 cents per word, cable count.

The above does not include the shipboard or shore station radio charge which must be added. There will be no charge on radiograms over the Signal Corps cable connecting Corregidor and Manila. (See examples for computing rates in paragraphs 71 c, d, and e.)

104 A. TABLE L.—*Rates through radio stations in the Hawaiian Islands.*

Mutual Telephone Co. (wireless department).

Ship to shore messages "Via Wahiawa" to any point on the islands of Oahu, Hawaii, Maui, Kauai, or Molokai, 10 cents a word.

Cablegrams or trans-Pacific radiograms will be accepted at the above rate *plus* the forwarding charges of the cable or wireless company *beyond* Honolulu. Messages of this class may be routed *via* "Commercial Cable," "Federal," or "Marconi" at the option of the sender.

The Mutual Telephone Co.'s shore rate is based on a 10-word minimum, cable count.

The rates to points *beyond* Honolulu, except to points enumerated in the first paragraph, are based on a flat word rate, cable count, no minimum.

Press rate to points enumerated in the first paragraph is 5 cents per word, 10-word minimum.

STATIONS OF MUTUAL TELEPHONE CO. (LTD.) (WIRELESS DEPARTMENT).

Station.	Island.	Call.	Power.
Wahiawa	Oahu	K. H. K.	2 Kw.
Lihue	Kauai	K. H. M.	2 Kw.
Lahaina	Maui	K. H. L.	2 Kw.
Kaunakakai	Molokai	K. H. O.	½ Kw.
Kawaihae	Hawaii	K. H. N.	2 Kw.

Stations open 7 a. m., close 5.30 p. m.

LONG-DISTANCE STATION.

Station.	Island.	Call.	Power.
Wahiawa	Oahu	K. H. K.	10 Kw.

Open day and night.

Commercial Cable Co. (Honolulu).

Radiograms intended for transmission via cable *beyond* Honolulu should be marked and routed "Via Cable-Honolulu."

The rate from Honolulu to San Francisco is 25 cents per word. For rates to points beyond San Francisco consult Postal Telegraph-Cable Co.'s Tariff Book, pages 795–813 for foreign points and page 821 for points in the United States and Canada.

These rates are based on a flat word rate, cable count, no minimum.

Federal Wireless Co.

Station for working with the United States only is situated at Heeia, island of Oahu. The radio rate from Heeia to San Francisco is 25 cents per word.

The rate to points beyond San Francisco is as follows:

	Word.
Alameda, Oakland, Berkeley, and San Francisco, Cal	$0.25
California (other than San Francisco), Idaho, Nevada, Oregon, Utah, Washington	.29
Colorado, Kansas, Montana, Nebraska, New Mexico, North Dakota, South Dakota, Wyoming	.31
Alabama, Arizona, Arkansas, Illinois, Iowa, Kentucky, Louisiana, Michigan, Minnesota, Mississippi, Missouri, Ohio, Oklahoma, Tennessee, Texas, Wisconsin	.34
Connecticut, Delaware, District of Columbia, Florida, Georgia, Maine, Maryland, Massachusetts, New Hampshire, New York, New Jersey, North Carolina, South Carolina, Pennsylvania, Vermont, Virginia, West Virginia	.37
England, Germany, France, Belgium	.62
Australia	.69
Saskatchewan	.37
Alberta	.37
Vancouver	.33
Victoria	.33

For rates to points not shown above use the rate to San Francisco, 25 cents, and add rate from San Francisco to destination as shown in Western Union Tariff Book.

These rates are based on a flat word rate, cable count, no minimum, and are for either day or night service.

This company does a strictly commercial business, working with San Francisco almost continually from 8 a. m. to 11.30 p. m. All traffic is delivered to the Western Union at San Francisco for additional transmission to points beyond.

Marconi Wireless Co.

Receiving station for radiograms is situated at Kohohead, island of Oahu.

Sending station for radiograms at Kahuku, island of Oahu.

These stations will handle business only with San Francisco and Japan, *but will not handle business with Army transports.*

Operators on Army transports routing business to San Francisco and Japan and points beyond "via Marconi" should transmit the same to Wahiawa (Mutual) and ascertain by service message the word rate from Wahiawa to destination.

The above rates do not include the ship radio charge, which must be added.

CHAPTER III.

CLASSIFICATION OF MESSAGES.

(Paragraphs 105 to 157.)

CHAPTER III.

CLASSIFICATION OF MESSAGES.

MESSAGES CLASSIFIED.

105. All messages accepted for transmission shall be classified as follows, and should be transmitted and accounted for in the manner indicated:

Class A. OFM—Official Business, War Department.

Class B. OFM—Official Business, other departments of the Government than the War Department.

Class C. OFM—Hydrographic and weather reports.

Class D. RADIO—Personal and commercial messages carrying tolls.

Class E. MSG—Free messages (D. H.).

Class F. SVC—Service messages.

PRIORITY OF TRANSMISSION.

106. As a general rule, transmission of all messages will be made in the order indicated above.

107. In very exceptional cases, and within the discretion of the chief radio operator, messages of classes D, E, and F of an urgent character may be given precedence in transmission over ordinary and routine messages of classes A, B, and C.

108. Messages of each class should be transmitted in the order of their filing except that when a message is of great importance or of such value that its value would be lost if delayed, the word "Rush" may be added to the prefix. Storm warnings shall always be so marked. Care should be taken that this designation is not placed on other than very important matter not admitting of delay.

OFFICIAL MESSAGES.

109. *Except as provided in paragraph 112-A,* all official messages of the officers and agents of the several departments of the United States Government are transmitted free over the military telegraph lines when properly certified, and this will also apply to the United States Army Radio Service.

110. Whenever properly certified messages are presented for transmission and a doubt exists as to their being on official business, or the genuineness of the party presenting them, they will be transmitted and a copy submitted to the zone officer in whose zone the station is located.

111. In accepting official messages for transmission over the Washington-Alaska Military Cable and Telegraph System it is essential that the following certificate be stamped or written on the message blank, when not already printed thereon, and same signed by the sender of the message, who will also indicate his rank and department or bureau of the Government to which the message pertains:

"I certify that the following telegram is on official business and necessary for the public service and will not bear the delay incident to the mails."

This will also apply to the United States Army Radio Service.

112. Official messages of the United States Government which pass in part over commercial lines or "other line" ships under the control of the United States will be entered on the "Monthly abstract of official messages accepted, etc." (Form 154). The original messages will be forwarded with this abstract at the end of the month to the zone officer in whose zone the ship or station is located, who will make disposition thereof by transferring them to the commercial companies concerned in lieu of a cash settlement for any "other line" charges.

112 A. Radiograms on Government business will carry the abbreviation "Govt.", which will *immediately precede* the address and be paid for, the tolls on such Government messages over the telegraph lines and cables which have accepted the provisions of the Act of 1866 relating to telegraph companies being subject to the rates fixed by the Postmaster General. (Order No. 7887, P. M. G., March 12, 1914.)

The Navy Department advises that the extensive chain of radio shore stations comprising the Navy Coast Signal Service is available to the officials of the War and other departments for the free transmission of all radiograms on official business from shore to ship, ship to shore, or ship to ship, plus any connecting line charges.

The above will also apply to the Army Coast Radio Stations in Alaska and at Corregidor, P. I.; also all Army transports equipped with radio apparatus, *except* that on and after July 1, 1914, all radiograms passing over the Washington-Alaska Military Cable and Telegraph System, on account of the departments of the Federal Government, other than the War Department, will bear a charge of one-half the established commercial rates for that system; no minimum, address and signature counted, plus any connecting line charges.

113. Official messages of the United States Government which are transmitted from a ship or station of the United States Army Radio Service direct to a ship or station under the control of a foreign government signatory to the international convention will be treated as indicated in paragraph 112, except that upon receipt of the original messages by the zone officer they will be forwarded to the Chief

Signal Officer of the Army for disposition in connection with the settlement of the foreign station's charges. All such messages should show clearly on their face the official name and address of the foreign ship or company to whom the "other line" charges fall.

114. Official messages of foreign governments will be accepted and accounted for as indicated for Class D (RADIO) messages; they will, however, be given precedence in transmission over personal or commercial messages of this class.

HYDROGRAPHIC AND WEATHER REPORTS.

115. For the benefit of shipping, the Naval Radio Service furnishes certain information and services gratis.

116. The time signal is transmitted from certain stations on the Atlantic and Pacific coasts of the continental United States, as shown in Appendix II.

117. At 8.00 a. m., noon, 4.00 p. m., and 8.00 p. m., coast naval radio stations send broadcast any hydrographic information concerning wrecks, derelicts, ice, or other dangers to navigation.

118. At certain times, which vary with the locality, the coast stations also send weather reports and forecasts furnished by the Weather Bureau. The coast stations also receive weather reports sent by ships to the Weather Bureau at Washington. Storm warnings are sent by coast stations whenever received. The lightship stations (Nantucket Shoals, Diamond Shoals, and Frying Pan Shoals) copy the weather reports and storm warnings and furnish them to passing ships upon request. (See Appendix III.)

119. The radio stations on the Nantucket Shoals and Diamond Shoals lightships will transmit, without charge, to Newport and Beaufort stations, respectively, messages from the masters of passing ships to their owners, agents, or maritime agency, giving notice of their passing. In all such cases arrangements must be made beforehand by such owners or agents for the forwarding of messages by land telegraph from the naval coast station to point of destination.

PERSONAL AND COMMERCIAL MESSAGES.

120. Additional to the regular type of commercial prepaid message (RADIO) the special types given below are authorized. The following list gives the names of these special types and also the abbreviated designations by which they are known:

Classes of messages:	Designations.
Radiograms with answer prepaid (on land lines, "Reply prepaid")	*RP
Radiograms calling for repetition of message (on land lines, "Repeat back")	*TC

* These designations are sent as supplementary instructions at the end of the preamble, separated from what goes before by the double dash, and again as the first item of the address. The two transmissions are separated by the double dash. On telegraph forms they are written just before the address. On radio blanks they are entered in the space marked "Special prefix."

Classes of messages—Continued.	Designations.
Special delivery radiograms	*EXPRESS
Radiograms to be delivered by mail	*POST
Radiograms to be delivered by registered mail	*PR
Multiple radiograms	*TM..x..
Radiograms calling for acknowledgment of receipt	*PCP (by mail) *PC (by telegraph)
Acknowledgment of above	CR
Paid service notices	RADIO ST (prefix)
"Ocean letters" or radiograms to be mailed by a ship at a port of call	POSTE (in address)

121. The following types of messages are not allowed as radiograms:

Telegraph money orders.

Telegrams at reduced rates for night letters, deferred cablegrams, etc.

Urgent telegrams, to take precedence over regular telegraphic traffic.

The last class, "urgent telegrams," is allowed on European systems but not in North America.

RADIOGRAMS WITH ANSWER PREPAID.

122. These contain the abbreviated instruction "RP....," the dots standing for the amount paid for return message. This expression is transmitted in two places, (1) as supplementary instructions at the end of the preamble; (2) as the first item in the address. The two transmissions are therefore separated by the double dash. The expression is transmitted free in the supplementary instructions, but is charged for in the address. The whole expression "RP...." (including the amount), sent in the address, is counted in the check as ONE word, and is charged for.

On radiogram blanks the expression shall be written in the "Special Prefix" space, and on telegraph blanks it shall be written just before the address.

123. By international convention the value of the reply message is to be expressed in francs, and in sending by radio to FOREIGN ships it shall be so expressed. In sending to United States ships it shall be expressed in dollars and cents. For conversion a franc shall be taken as equal to 20 cents United States currency. For example: "RP fr 14" would be sent in a message to a foreign ship, and "RP two dollars eighty" to a United States ship. Fractional amounts in francs are expressed thus: Fr. 18.60; in United States currency the amount may be expressed thus: Dols. 3.72.

124. On land lines of the United States the value of the reply is expressed by the number of words prepaid for such reply. There-

* These designations are sent as supplementary instructions at the end of the preamble, separated from what goes before by the double dash, and again as the first item of the address. The two transmissions are separated by the double dash. On telegraph forms they are written just before the address. On radio blanks they are entered in the space marked "Special prefix."

fore, in forwarding a radiogram from a ship to the land lines, the operator in charge of the coast station shall convert the money value, as given by the ship, into the equivalent number of words. This will necessitate the operator's knowing all charges accurately, and care must be used in making the conversion.

125. NOTE THAT THE 10-WORD MINIMUM CHARGE APPLIES TO THE REPLY MESSAGE.

126. Similarly, when a reply prepaid message is received at a coast station from land lines for transmission to a ship, the value of the reply message must be converted from the number of words into the money equivalent, francs or dollars. In case of doubt as to the rate, send a service message to ascertain it.

127. The receiver of a reply prepaid message is given a voucher equal in value to the amount prepaid for reply. This voucher is good for six weeks only. *The receiver of such a message on shipboard is not bound to send a reply to the sender of the original message, but may apply the value of his voucher to the payment of any message he wishes to send.* Should the expression "Reply prepaid," or, on foreign messages, "Réponse payée" be used instead of RP, the operator shall transmit it by the abbreviation RP; but it is to be noted that in cases where the full expression is transmitted by other stations, each word in it is charged. The prepaid answer to such a message is, in reality, a paid message, and is so treated. On land lines in the United States the prefix "Collect reply" is used by the Western Union Co. and "Anstorp" by the Postal Co.; but for radio work no special prefix is necessary. The word "Radio" in the preamble indicates that the message is a commercial paid message.

RADIOGRAMS CALLING FOR REPETITION OF MESSAGE.

128. Such repetition is for the purpose of verification only. In this case the expression "TC" or the words "repeat back" are used. The expression "TC" is transmitted as supplementary instructions at the end of the preamble, and also as the first item of the address, in the same manner as described for the expression "RP . . . ." under the heading "Radiograms with answer prepaid," which see. This expression in the address is counted in the check as ONE word and is charged for. In this case the message is repeated back by each station that relays it to the one before. The additional charge for repeating back is one-fourth of the regular tolls. Should the expression "repeat back" be written by the sender, it shall be transmitted by the abbreviation "TC."

SPECIAL DELIVERY RADIOGRAMS.

129. These are messages which involve delivery beyond the limits of a telegraph office. Such delivery is accomplished by messenger or telephone. The international convention stipulates that these shall be accepted only in cases where the charge for special delivery is paid by the addressee. The special prefix for this class of messages is "EXPRESS," sent as supplementary instructions at the end of the preamble; and again as the first item of the address, the same as stated above for the expression "RP . . . . ." The word "EXPRESS" in the address is counted in the check and is charged as ONE word.

RADIOGRAMS TO BE DELIVERED BY MAIL.

130. These are distinguished by the service instruction "POST," transmitted as supplementary instructions at the end of the preamble and again as the first item of the address. Such radiograms shall be sent by mail by the coast station receiving them, to the addressee; or, if the name of some other place follows the word "POST," shall be forwarded by land line to that place with the instruction "Mail." It is then mailed from the telegraph office to which forwarded. An additional charge of one word is made for the instruction "POST" (and it is counted in the check), and five cents ($0.05) for postage. The expression "PR" used instead of "POST," signifies that the letter is to be forwarded by registered mail. In this case the charges must include fifteen cents ($0.15) for postage instead of five cents ($0.05).

Foreign ships may use "Poste recommandée," or, "Registered post," in lieu of "PR." In such case each word of the expression is counted and charged.

MULTIPLE RADIOGRAMS.

131. By multiple radiogram is meant one message addressed either to several persons, or to the same person at several addresses, in the same locality or in different localities served by the same telegraph office. Such messages contain the abbreviation "TM x" ("x" standing for the number of different addresses). This is transmitted by radio as supplementary instructions at the end of the preamble and also as the first item of the first address. The "TM x" in the address is counted in the check, for radio transmission. It is not forwarded over the land lines. Multiple telegrams are not recognized as such by land lines in the United States; therefore, such a message is charged for as so many different messages, and must be so put on the land wires. That is, a multiple message may be received by radio, the various addresses being followed by but one "body of message" or text. When put on the land lines each message would have to be complete; i. e., the text accompanies each address, each separate message on a separate blank. This will involve special care in determining the charges on a multiple message.

RADIOGRAMS CALLING FOR ACKNOWLEDGMENT OF RECEIPT.

132. Such acknowledgment is limited to notification of the date and hour at which the coast station shall have transmitted the radiogram to the ship to which it was addressed. This notification is sent to the office of origin either by telegraph or mail, at the option of the sender of the message. The instruction to send acknowledgment of receipt is transmitted by the letters "PC," or the words "Acknowledgment Paid," as supplementary instructions at the end of the preamble, and also as the first item of the first address. The letters "PC" in the address are counted in the check and charged for as one word. This calls for telegraphic acknowledgment. The letters "PCP" instead of "PC" call for acknowledgment by mail, and are charged for as one word. Should the expression "Acknowledgment Paid" be written on the blank, it shall be transmitted by the abbreviation.

If telegraphic acknowledgment is requested, the sender of the message is charged for a five-word telegram, by the same route. Mail acknowledgments are sent free. They are addressed to the telegraph office at which the message originated. Telegraphic acknowledgment is announced by service message containing the abbreviation "CR," followed by the name of the addressee, ship, the word "transmitted," and the hour and date. Example: Jupiter, having received a radiogram from Lincoln, Nebr., for Jones on the ship *Regina*, and transmitted it at 10.00 a. m., on the 25th of the month, sends the following telegram to the land-line office at Lincoln:

"CR Jones *Regina* transmitted 10 a. 25"

PAID SERVICE NOTICES.

133. These are service messages—i. e., messages exchanged only between OFFICES (stations), whether radio or telegraph—sent at the request of a sender of a commercial message, and are charged for at regular rates. The London Convention prohibits paid service messages calling for repetition or information. Paid service messages are designated by the prefix "RADIO ST" instead of "RADIO." They may be sent for various reasons, as, to rectify or complete an address; to rectify or complete the text; to cancel a message. (See paragraphs 143–157 for forms.)

OCEAN LETTERS.

(Radiograms to be Mailed by a Ship at a Port of Call.)

134. Radiograms may be transmitted by a coast station to a ship, or by a ship to another ship, to be forwarded by mail from a port of call of the ship receiving the radiogram. These are known as "Ocean Letters." Such radiograms shall not be entitled to any relaying by radio. The address of such a radiogram shall embrace the following:

(1) The paid designation "Poste" or (if sent to a United States ship) "Mail," followed by name of port at which message is to be mailed.

(2) Name and complete address of addressee.

(3) Name of station on shipboard by which radiogram is to be mailed.

(4) When necessary, the name of the coast station.

135. The address shall be broken by transmitting the double dash AFTER the name of the port at which the ocean letter is to be mailed. These words form part of the address none the less.

EXAMPLE.

A radiogram sent via the Jupiter coast station for transmission to the S. S. *Avon*, to be mailed by her at Buenos Aires, would be addressed as follows:

"Poste Buenos Aires=Suarez 14 Calle Prat Valparaiso Avon Jupiter."

The rate shall comprise, in addition to the radio and telegraph rates, a sum of five cents ($0.05) for postage.

FREE MESSAGES.

136. This class of message is established for the purpose of giving officers and crews of Army transports, and the commissioned and enlisted personnel of the Army on board, special facilities in sending messages to their families and friends relating to matters of an *urgent personal nature,* concerning death, serious illness, or accident. Messages on semiofficial business, as requests for leave or change of duty, are also allowed under this class.

137. Similar messages addressed to an army ship board station, when filed at an Army land radio station, and sent by authorized persons (Par. 136), will be handled under the same conditions as if originating on board ship.

138. On these messages there are no ship-radio charges, nor coast-station charge when the coast station is also a station of the United States Army Radio Service, but the commercial radio-station charge and land-line tolls to destination must be fully prepaid. These charges are computed by cable rules, 10-word minimum, the same as for commercial radiograms (Class D). Such messages must be given SRS numbers in the ship's regular sequence, and must be specially marked and designated for radio transmission by the prefix "MSG" if they carry no tolls and "RADIO" if they carry coast-station or land-line charges. They may be relayed only so far as is necessary to reach the nearest coast station.

139. They must be duly authorized by the ship's master, relate only to such matters as are specified in paragraph 136, and be sent at such time as the ship's master may direct.

140. The originals of Class E messages, with full notations thereon, should be forwarded to the zone officer, as is required for all messages sent, received, or relayed, on which any charges whatever have been paid.

141. Replies to Class E messages, when sent by persons not entitled to free service, must be made through stations open to commercial business and full tolls applied.

142. The radio apparatus shall not be used for exchange of notes between operators, or for UNOFFICIAL WORK OF ANY KIND with the single exception of "MSG" messages, which must be authorized and handled in exact accordance with the foregoing.

SERVICE MESSAGES—PAID SERVICE MESSAGES.

143. Service messages may be sent on any subject connected with the handling or routing of messages, tariffs, charges, etc., and may be sent to any ship, coast station, or telegraph office with which a station has dealings.

144. Such messages have the prefix SVC (foreign ships use "A" followed by the word RADIO). They are sent between operators only, and in radio transmission are not addressed nor signed except by names of offices. On land lines they are addressed to the office concerned.

145. They should be made as brief as possible, and the special signals given in paragraphs 261–262 employed whenever possible. In communicating with commercial ships or stations no other abbreviations shall be used, as they would not be understood. No superfluous words or signals are permitted.

146. Service messages which relate strictly to commercial messages may be sent via any coast station, even though it belongs to a different system from that through which the paid message to which the service refers was sent. In exceptional cases, ships of other administrations may be used likewise for forwarding service messages.

147. SVC messages are not charged and do not enter into accounts, but copies of all SVC messages relating to any commercial (paid) message must be forwarded with the copy of commercial message to the zone officer, so as to present all facts bearing on the case and save further reference to the radio station concerned. Operators must be careful to distinguish between service (SVC) messages and paid service (RADIO ST) messages. The latter are treated in every way as regular commercial messages, but are sent to radio or telegraph offices only at request of the sender of a regular commercial message and upon payment by the sender.

148. Service messages are in form as follows:

— • — • —
Prefix (SVC).
Name of office of destination.
De (From).
Name of office of origin.
Number of service message.

— • • • —
Text.

— • • • —
Call letters of sending station.

149. The text of a service message contains:

(1) The number of the message to which it refers;

(2) The date on which that message was sent; (This date is written out, thus: twelfth, and is *not* expressed in figures);

(3) Name of addressee, or, in case of nondelivery, the *full* address. Then follows the communication.

150. The following examples of service messages will serve to show their form as well as customary wording:

(1) Ship *Regina* (KSA) has received a message from Omaha via NAR addressed Williams. No such addressee can be found. The ship then sends the following:

— • — • —
SVC
Omaha
De (From).
Regina
1
— • • • —
2 (Number of NAR's undelivered message).
Twelfth (date of NAR's undelivered message).
Williams (addressee of NAR's undelivered message).
Not on board.
• — • — •
KSA
— • —

(2) NAR having received notice of nondelivery of message sent by ship *Regina* (KSA) on the tenth via NAP to Albany, signals:

— • — • —
SVC
Regina
De (From).
Albany
1
— • • • —

Yours tenth Wilson no sig undelivered. Give better address.

. — . — .

NAR

— . —

151. Should a ship receive a service indicating that an error had been made in transmitting the address, it shall send a service in reply correcting same.

152. Coast stations shall use the phrase "Ship out of range" in service messages sent inland to signify that a ship for which a message is received has already passed, and "Ship not signaled" to indicate a message has been held eight days for a ship and she has not yet been communicated with.

PAID SERVICE MESSAGES.

153. These differ from the above only in the fact that they are sent at the request of a sender of a regular message, and are paid for at regular rates. They have the prefix RADIO ST. To promote uniformity, the phraseology of such messages shall follow the examples given below, when they will serve the purpose.

154. The restrictions on paid service messages given in paragraph 133 must be carefully observed.

CORRECTION OF ADDRESS.

155. When a sender wishes to correct or complete the address of a radiogram which has failed of delivery, a paid service message may be sent.

EXAMPLE.

2 fourteenth Jones deliver 8 Dey Street.

This change means: Change address on my message number two of the fourteenth addressed Jones to 8 Dey Street.

CORRECTION OF TEXT.

156. A sender may correct the text of a message by sending a paid service message.

EXAMPLE.

2 fourteenth Jones replace duplex by simplex.

This means: In my message number two of the fourteenth change word "duplex" to "simplex."

CANCELING A MESSAGE.

157. A sender may endeavor to cancel a message before it is delivered to the addressee, by sending a paid service message.

EXAMPLE.

2 fourteenth Jones cancel.

If the message has already been delivered, the addressee will be notified of its cancellation. Should the sender wish to know whether his original message was delivered, he must send his paid service message as a reply prepaid message also, in which case the office of destination will reply:

"Yours Jones unsigned canceled"

(or)

"Yours Jones already delivered."

Prepayment must be made for a 10-word reply.

CHAPTER IV.

LANGUAGE. COUNTING OF WORDS.

(Paragraphs 158 to 192.)

CHAPTER IV.

LANGUAGE—COUNTING OF WORDS.

LANGUAGE.

158. A radiogram may be sent in plain language, code language, or cipher; these languages may be used alone or conjointly.

(1) Radiograms in plain language are those composed of words, figures, and letters which offer an intelligible meaning in any of the European languages or Latin. The words and letters must be written in Roman characters. In case of unfamiliarity with the language being sent, the sending operator's statement that a message is in "plain language" shall be accepted. The presence of trade marks or of abbreviated expressions current in the country, as fob, cod, etc., does not alter the character of a plain language radiogram.

(2) Code language is composed of real words not forming intelligible phrases, or of artificial words consisting of pronounceable groups of letters, such as words in which the letters are alternately consonants and vowels. No code word, whether real or artificial, may exceed ten letters in length. The real words may be drawn from any of the following languages: English, French, German, Dutch, Italian, Spanish, Portuguese, and Latin. The artificial words must be formed of syllables which must be pronounceable according to the current usages of one of those languages. Combinations formed by running together two or more real words, whole or contracted, or a real word and some other expression are prohibited, e. g., atonce, safternoon, etc.

(3) Cipher is composed of (a) Arabic figures or groups, or series of Arabic figures having a secret meaning, or letters or groups, or a series of letters having a secret meaning; (b) Combinations of letters not fulfilling the conditions applicable to plain language or code.

Letter and figure cipher can not be combined in one group.

159. The mixture, in one group, of figures and letters having a secret meaning is not permitted. This prohibition does not include trade terms, e. g., IP76, as such are not considered as having secret meaning. Such expressions as 21dot13, used to express latitude or longitude, are likewise admitted.

COUNTING OF WORDS.

GENERAL.

160. The word system of counting shall be observed, and all words in the address, text, and signature must be counted and charged for.

161. No item in the preamble will be counted, but the abbreviated supplementary instructions, transmitted as the first item of the address in the case of radiograms of special classes (see Chapter III) shall be counted and charged as one word. If a route is designated in the address it shall not be counted or charged.

162. A message may contain any number of words at the option of the sender. No text or signature is required.

ADDRESS.

163. The address must consist of at least two words, the first indicating the name of the addressee, the second the "place to."

164. In the address of any message the names of the delivery office, counties, provinces, States, or other territorial subdivision and country are each counted as one word, without regard to the number of letters required to spell them; other proper names in addresses or signatures are counted at the rate of one word for every 15 letters or fraction thereof. Names of ships shall be counted as one word, irrespective of the number of letters in the address, and if in case of two or more ships of the same name the call letters are added, the name and call letters together are counted as one word. In the text of messages the names of ships are charged at the rate of 15 or 10 letters to the word if all parts are joined to form one word. (See pars. 170, 174, 179, 180.)

165. In the address if the name of the State is given, it is counted and charged for as one word, additional to the town.

166. When a message is addressed to the care of a person who has a registered address, the words "care" or "care of" (or the French form "chez"), or their equivalent, must be written before the registered address; thus a message for "Barnett, London," to be delivered to the registered address "Morgan, London," should be addressed, "Barnett, care (or 'care of') Morgan, London," or "Barnett chez Morgan, London."

167. The words *street, place, road, square,* and *park* are always to be counted each as one word, separately from the name of the street, place, road, square, and park, whether written together or apart.

168. Groups of letters, e. g., initials, must not be accepted in the address, but each letter is charged separately as one word. In house or street numbers, however, such groups are allowed; thus, 184th, 106A, 27ten (foreign), 42mo (foreign), 15bis (foreign).

169. In the case of a message destined for a ship, the name of the ship, together with its call letters (in the case of ships of which there are more than one with the same name listed in the Official List of Radiotelegraphic Stations), regardless of its length, counts as one word. Similarly, the name of the coast station counts as one word.

TEXT.

PLAIN LANGUAGE.

170. In a message written entirely in plain language the maximum length of chargeable words is fixed at 15 characters. Words of more than 15 characters are charged at the rate of one word for every 15 characters or fraction thereof.

171. Abbreviated and misspelled words, illegitimate compound words, or words combined in a manner contrary to the usage of a language are forbidden, but if they should accidentally appear in a radiogram they will be counted and charged at the rate of one word for every five letters or fraction thereof.

172. Nevertheless, the names of *towns* and *countries;* surnames belonging to one person; names of places, squares, boulevards, streets, and other public thoroughfares; and names of ships, may be written as one word and charged at the rate of 15 characters to the word (in plain messages).

173. Words joined by a hyphen or separated by an apostrophe are counted as so many separate words.

CODE LANGUAGE.

174. In code messages the maximum length of the chargeable word is fixed at 10 characters.

175. Code words of more than 10 letters must be counted and charged at cipher rate—that is, five letters to a word—and noted in the check; but genuine words of more than 10 letters may be used in their original sense, and may be counted at the rate of 10 letters to the word.

176. Combinations or alterations of words concealed by reversing the order of the letters or syllables will not be accepted as code words.

CIPHER LANGUAGE.

177. In cipher, the letters or figures in each uninterrupted series shall be counted at the rate of five, or a fraction of five, as one word. Groups of letters are charged at the same rate as groups of figures, but figures and letters must be counted separately; thus A5C counts as three words (but see "trade-marks" below).

29732°—14——5

MIXED LANGUAGE.

178. In messages written in code and plain language, the maximum length of word chargeable is 10 characters.

179. In messages containing plain language and cipher the words in passages in plain language are charged at the rate of one word for every 15 characters or fraction thereof, and the groups in the passages in cipher language at the rate of one word for every five characters or fraction thereof.

180. In messages written in plain language, code language, and cipher language, the words in the passages in plain language and code language are charged as code language, and the passages in cipher language are charged as cipher language.

MISCELLANEOUS.

181. Numbers, whether whole or fractional, expressed in words written so that each number or group of numbers forms one continuous word may be counted and charged for at the rate of 15 or 10 letters, or a fraction of 15 or 10 letters, to a word. (See paragraphs 170, 174, 179, 180.)

182. Roman numbers can not be produced by the Morse Code. (V, VII, XIX, etc.) Senders should be requested to substitute Arabic figures or words.

183. Signs of punctuation, hyphens, apostrophes, and fresh paragraphs are not counted or sent except upon formal demand of the sender, in which case they will be charged for as one word each.

184. Inverted commas, the two signs of the parentheses, and each *separate* figure, letter, initial, or underline will be counted as one word. Groups of figures will be counted at the rate of five figures, or fraction thereof, as one word.

185. Groups of letters forming commercial trade-marks or expressions in current use, as COD, FOB, OK, AM, PM, RR, USS, SS, should be counted at the rate of five letters or figures to a word. Periods, hyphens, or dashes, and bars of division used in the formation of fractional or other numbers, or in commercial marks or similar expressions, are each to be counted as a letter in the groups in which they occur. Letters and figures may also be combined in one group *in commercial marks,* otherwise letters must be counted separately from figures.

186. Groups of letters shall not be accepted in the address. All letters other than those forming names or words shall, in the address, be separated and charged for as one word each. They are then transmitted as separate words.

187. Decimal points and commas used in the formation of numbers and letters added to figures to form ordinal numbers, or to represent the number of a house, are each to be counted as a figure and charged for at the rate of five figures or a fraction thereof as one word.

188. In code words of trade-marks, the letters ae, aa, ao, oe, ue are to be counted as two letters each.

189. When the letters *ch* come together in the spelling of the genuine word they are counted as one letter. They are counted separately in artificial code words and cipher words.

190. Code words or groups of letters or trade-marks must not contain the accented letters ä, á, å, é, ñ, ö, ü.

191. In sending the number of words as the check, if the actual number of words in the message is not the same as the number of words charged for, the number is signaled as a fraction, the numerator indicating the number of words charged for, the denominator the actual number of words, thus:

15 — · · — · 13

192. *Examples of counting.*

	Words in text.	Words in address.
Responsibility (14 letters)	1	....
Unconstitutional (16 letters)	2	....
A-t-il (French)	3	....
Aujourdhui (French)	1	....
Aujourd'hui (French)	2	....
Newyork	1	1
New York	2	1
New South Wales	3	1
Newsouthwales	1	1
Frankfort Main	2	1
Frankfurt am Main	3	1
Frankfurt a-/M	3	1
Frankfurtmain	1	1
Starokonstantinow (town in Russia)	2	1
Emmingen Hannover	2	1
Emmingen Wurtemberg	2	1
Van de Brande	3	3
Vandebrande	1	1
Dubois	1	1
Du Bois	2	2
Hyde Park	2	2
Hydepark (contrary to usage)	2	2
Hydepark Square[1]	2	2
Saintjames Street	2	2
Saint James Street	3	3
State of Maryland (name of ship)	3	1
Stateofmaryland (name of ship)	1	1
Emvthf (cipher)	2	....
Sextyzlergs (cipher)	3	....
398499 (cipher)	2	....
441/2 (5 figures and signs)	1	1
137th	1	1
1374th	2	2
108 A (number of house)	1	1
444,55 (six figures and signs)	2	....
46.221	2	....
100 dollars	2	....
One hundred dollars	3	....
Onehundred dollars	2	....

[1] In this case the expression "Hydepark," written as a single word, counts as one word, because the word "park" forms an integral part of the name of the square.

Examples of counting—Continued.

	Words in text.	Words in address.
10 fr. 50	3	
11h30	3	
44/2	1	
2%	1	
Two hundred and thirty four	5	
Twohundredand thirtyfour	2	
$\frac{ap}{m}$ (trade-mark)	1	
$\frac{3}{m}$ (trade-mark)	1	
CHF 45 (trade-mark)	1	
(no doubt)		
"no doubt"	3	
'no doubt'		
totally (underlined)	2	
incontrovertibility (underlined)	3	
allright, alright (contrary to usage)	2	
The business is urgent start at once (7 words and 2 underlines)	9	

CHAPTER V.

OPERATION. TRANSMISSION OF MESSAGES. SPECIAL SIGNALS.

(Paragraphs 193 to 301.)

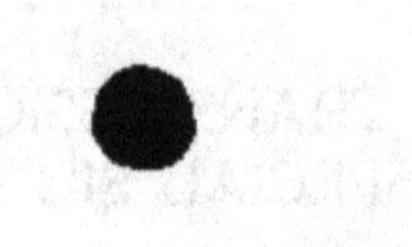

CHAPTER V.

OPERATION—TRANSMISSION OF MESSAGES—SPECIAL SIGNALS.

POWER.

193. All stations must communicate with the minimum power to effect reliable communication. Commercial ships are forbidden to use more than 1 kilowatt of power at generator terminals under normal circumstances and when within 200 miles of the nearest coast station.

194. Every station which has occasion to transmit a radiogram requiring the use of high power shall first send out three times the signal of warning — — . . — — with the minimum of power necessary to reach the neighboring stations. It shall not begin to transmit with high power until 5 seconds after sending the signal of warning.

CODE.

195. The International Morse Code shall be used exclusively.

WAVE LENGTHS.

196. Two wave lengths, one of 600 meters and the other of 300 meters, are authorized for general public service. All Army stations, ship and coast, must use these wave lengths when communicating with commercial ships or commercial coast stations. In general, the standard length used is 600 meters, and all stations opened to commercial work are prepared to use that length. Such stations may listen in on that wave length for at least 5 minutes every quarter hour, except when engaged in communication on other wave lengths, in which case they must cease every 15 minutes and listen in for 3 minutes on 600 meters. A wave length of 1,800 meters is authorized for certain communication, as explained in paragraph 273.

CALL AND REPLY.

197. As a general rule it is the ship which calls the shore station, and ships coming within range of a shore station should call the station, whether they have messages to send or not.

CALL.

198. The call is composed of the attention signal — . — . — followed by the call letters of the station called, repeated three times, then by "DE," followed by the call letters of the calling station, repeated three times.

199. To call a ship or station within range, whose call is not known, or to ascertain if any station is within range, use CQ

— . — .   — — . —

in place of call letters of station called.

EXAMPLES.

(1) Ship KSA calls NAN

— . — . —

NAN NAN NAN

— . .   .

KSA KSA KSA

(2) Ship KSA desires to know whether any station is within range:

— . — . —

CQ CQ CQ

— . .   .

KSA KSA KSA

200. If a station does not answer the call transmitted three times at intervals of 2 minutes, the call shall not be resumed until after an interval of 15 minutes, the station issuing the call having first made sure of the fact that no radio correspondence is in progress.

DISTRESS CALL.

201. The distress call is . . . — — — . . . (SOS), which is substituted for the letters of the station called. It shall be answered by any ship or station that hears it, unless there is added the call of some particular station, when that station alone shall reply. Any ship or station hearing a distress call shall cease all other radio work until the call is answered and the correspondence relating thereto is finished.

REPLY.

202. A station replies by making the attention signal — . — . — followed by the call letters of the calling station repeated three times, then "DE" — . .   . , its own call letters made once, ending with the "go ahead" signal — . — if ready to receive, otherwise with the "wait" signal . — . . . or one of the conventional abbreviations which fits the case.

203. Special care shall be taken not to interrupt the business of the station, which may be receiving signals at the time, which can not be received on board ship, on account of the lower aerial; the ship shall, therefore, cease calling promptly on demand.

EXAMPLES.

NAN having been called by KSA replies:

KSA KSA KSA

— . . .

NAN

— . —

(or — . — . —

KSA KSA KSA

— . . .

NAN

QRX

POSITION REPORTS.

204. As soon as the coast station has answered, the shipboard station shall furnish it with the following data in case it has messages to transmit; such data shall likewise be furnished upon request from the coast station. This report shall be preceded by the letters TR:

(a) The approximate distance, in nautical miles, of the vessel from the coast station.

(b) The position of the vessel indicated in a concise form and adapted to the circumstances of the case.

(c) Her next port of call.

(d) The number of radiograms, if the total number of words therein does not exceed 50, otherwise the number of words.

Items (a), (b), and (c) shall be obtained from authorized official sources.

The speed of the ship in nautical miles shall also be given if specially requested by the coast station.

EXAMPLE.

— . — . —

TR

50

Off Cape Canaveral

Veracruz

3

. — . — .

KSA

The various items may be designated by the signals QRB, etc.

205. The coast station shall acknowledge the position report, and state the number of radiograms to be transmitted to the ship, provided the total number of words therein does not exceed 50, otherwise it shall state the number of words it has to send, and also the order of transmission.

206. If the transmission can not take place immediately, the coast station shall inform the station on shipboard of the approximate length of time that it will be necessary to wait.

207. If a shipboard station called can not receive for the moment, it shall inform the station calling of the approximate length of time that it will be necessary to wait.

208. In the exchange of messages between two stations on shipboard it shall fall to the station called to fix the order of transmission.

209. When a coast station receives calls from several shipboard stations, it shall decide the order in which such stations shall be admitted to exchange their messages.

210. In fixing this order the coast station shall be guided exclusively by the necessity of permitting each station concerned to exchange the greatest possible number of radiograms.

211. The coast station, in fixing the order of transmission, uses the word "series," or "alternate," or the appropriate abbreviated signal, as suits the case.

212. The following examples show the form in which the coast station acknowledges the position report, and fixes the order of transmission:

EXAMPLES.

(1) NAR acknowledging position report of ship KSA:

KSA
. — .
TR
50 series 3
. — . — .

This indicates that NAR has 50 words to send to KSA, and that transmission shall be made in series of 3 messages. The signal . — . — . means that NAR has closed off from sending, simply to receive KSA's acknowledgment, after which NAR will resume sending.

(2) KSA
. — .
TR
50 QSF
. — . — .

This means, "I have 50 words to transmit to you. Transmission to be alternately. I shall begin after you acknowledge."

(3) KSA
. — .
TR
50 QSF
— . —

This means the same as example (2), except that KSA is told to go ahead and send its first message.

(4) KSA
. — .
TR
50
. — . . .
. . — —
. — . — .

This means, "I have 50 words to transmit to you. Stand by for 20 minutes." (Note the use of the abbreviated numeral signals; these would be used by a European coast station, but are *not* to be used by the U. S. Army Radio Service.)

The ship acknowledges thus:

NAR
. — .
KSA
Operator's sign.

TRANSMISSION OF MESSAGES.

213. The transmission of every message shall be preceded by the ATTENTION signal.

214. When a message to be sent contains more than 40 words, the sending ship or station shall interrupt the transmission after each series of about 20 words with an interrogation

. . — — . .

and shall not continue until the receiving station repeats the last word received and

— . —

or, if transmission is very good, just the signal — . —

215. In the case of transmission by series, acknowledgment of receipt shall be made after each radiogram.

216. Coast stations engaged in the transmission of long radiograms shall suspend the transmission at the end of each period of 15 minutes, and remain silent for a period of 3 minutes before resuming the transmission.

217. Every message comprises the following:

Attention signal — . — . —

Preamble.

Supplementary instructions (if any).

Address (and route, if any).

Text.

Signature.

End of message.

Sending station call (sent only at end of last message, if a series is being sent).

PREAMBLE.

218. The preamble consists of all the items sent before the address. It follows the ATTENTION signal

— • — • —

and is followed by the BREAK or DOUBLE DASH

— • • • —

which separates it from the supplementary instructions, or address, as the case may be.

219. The preamble consists of:

Prefix,

Office of destination,

De,

Office of origin,

No. of message,

Operator's sign,

Check,

Date and hour of filing,

Via .... (Insert name of last relaying ship or coast station, if message is relayed.)

PREFIX.

220. The prefix for any commercial radiogram is the word "RADIO." That for a paid-service message is "RADIO ST." For regular service messages between operators "SVC" is used. In the case of a message whose text is framed in the International Signal Code, the letters "PRB" shall follow the word "RADIO."

OFFICES OF DESTINATION AND OF ORIGIN.

221. These shall be transmitted by *name.* Where ambiguity may be caused by the ship's name, it is permissible to add her call letters to the name, but ordinarily the name will suffice. By offices of destination and origin are meant the places to which the message is destined and at which it originated. They may be ship stations, coast stations, or land telegraph offices. These names shall always be transmitted, even though one of the stations (the transmitting or receiving station) be office of origin or destination. The examples given hereafter illustrate their use.

NUMBER OF MESSAGE.

222. Each message, regardless of class, sent by a ship or station, will be numbered in sequence, the first message of each day sent to a certain ship, station, or land-line office, to be numbered "1." This number is known as the "station" number. Each ship or station will have a separate series of numbers for each station or land-line office to which it transmits, a new series beginning each day at midnight.

223. The receiving number is that given by the ship, station, or office received from, and will not be transmitted; but a new number will be assigned, in case the message is retransmitted, which will be the next number in sequence for the station sent to. The number will be transmitted immediately after the name of office of origin without the abbreviation "No." or "Nr." In receiving a series of messages, the sequence of the numbers will be noted, and in case a break in the sequence should occur, inquiry for the missing message shall be made immediately.

EXAMPLES.

(1) The first ten messages received at a station on a certain day are from the *S. S. Amazon.* They should be numbered 1–10 by the *Amazon.* The next two messages are from the REID, numbered 1 and 2 by the REID.

(2) The next messages from the REID are sent to the LOUISIANA direct. They should also be numbered 1 and 2 by the REID.

(3) All of the messages received by the station from the *Amazon* and the REID are turned over to a land-line or cable office for further transmission with the numbers 1–12, being the first messages sent that date through that office.

S. R. S. NUMBER.

224. For the purpose of accounting, each commercial (including paid service) message is given a number known as the S. R. S. number, but this number *is never transmitted by radio nor over telegraph or cable lines.* Relayed commercial messages are given an S. R. S. number, followed by capital letter R. All service messages sent concerning a commercial message are given the S. R. S. number of the message to which they refer, followed by small letter "a" for the first service, "b" for the second, and so on. (See paragraph 55.)

OPERATOR'S SIGN.

225. The sending operator's sign shall follow the number of message and shall be recorded on the sending message blank. No operator shall change his personal sign without the authority of the electrician-in-charge of the station, or the radio or signal officer on board ship. No two operators at a station or on board a ship shall use the same sign. No operator shall use the letters K or R, nor any combination including one of these letters, for his sign.

CHECK.

226. The check shall consist of the number of words included in the address, text and signature, counted according to the rules given herein. (See Chapter IV.) In the case of supplementary instructions being sent, those included in the address are included in the counting of words for the check. The specification of route in the address is not counted. The number, or numbers, only, shall be sent, without the indication "Ck."

DATE AND HOUR OF FILING.

227. In the case of a commercial message filed on board ship, the date and hour of filing *shall always be transmitted* to the coast station. The date is expressed by the day of the month, written out, thus, *tenth*, followed by the hour (in figures) and the letters am or pm.

228. A coast station will, however, not forward the date and hour of filing when placing a message on the land lines, as the land-line companies in the United States do not transmit this information free. Similarly, a message received by a coast station from the land lines will not contain this item, so that a coast station in the United States never transmits it to a ship. Note shall be made, however, on the sending blank of a coast station, showing the date and hour of forwarding it, as well as date and hour of receiving it. This information is for use of the zone officer.

RELAYING SHIPS OR COAST STATIONS.

229. If a commercial message from a ship were relayed by two ships, the second would insert "Via," followed by the call letters of the first relaying ship. This information is not forwarded over the land lines by the coast station. (See paragraphs 281–288 for instructions for forwarding messages by land lines.) Likewise, if a message to a ship were relayed by a ship, the relaying ship would send the call letters of coast station after the word "Via."

230. The above items, constituting the preamble, are followed by the BREAK — . . . —

SUPPLEMENTARY INSTRUCTIONS.

231. These are sent only in the case of special classes of radiograms (see Chapter III); they are transmitted twice; first, as supplementary instructions, following the preamble, from which they are separated by the double dash; and, second, as the first item of the address. For further instructions on this subject see Chapter III.

232. When supplementary instructions are sent, they are followed by the BREAK _ . . . _

232 A. Radiograms on Government business will carry the abbreviation "Govt.", which will be the last word of the address and be paid for, the tolls on such Government messages over the telegraph lines and cables which have accepted the provisions of the act of 1866 relating to telegraph companies being subject to the rates fixed by the Postmaster General. (Order No. 7887, P. M. G., March 12, 1914.)

THE ADDRESS AND ROUTE.

233. The address of a commercial message for a destination ashore must consist of at least two words: The name of the addressee, and the name of the telegraph office of destination. Telegraph companies will register radio addresses at all offices without charge.

234. The address of radiograms intended *for ships* shall be as complete as possible; it shall embrace the following:

(a) The name or title of the addressee, with additional designations, if any.

(b) The name of the vessel as it appears in the first column of the list of radio stations of the world.

(c) The name of the coast station as it appears in the list.

235. It should be noted that, in cases where there are two or more ships of the same name, the call letters should follow the name and are considered part of it, the name and call letters together being charged as one word in the address.

236. Besides the address proper, certain other items are transmitted when they occur, with the address. These are:

(a) Designation of special type of radiogram.—If the radiogram is one of the special types described in Chapter III, the designation of the type, besides being transmitted in the supplementary instructions, is transmitted as the *first* item of the address.

(b) Where there is a choice of routes which the message may follow after reaching the coast, the sender may designate the one he prefers. In this case the route, in concise form, following the word "Via" is transmitted at the end of the address.

237. The address is followed by the BREAK _ . . . _

TEXT OF MESSAGE.

238. The text of message, and signature, if any, must be sent exactly as received. The address, message, and signature must be sent with special care, the sending operator regulating his speed to suit the ability of the receiving operator, avoiding a jerky style of sending. Messages containing code words or cipher should be sent more slowly than those entirely in plain language.

239. Any marks of punctuation, abbreviation, etc., written by the sender, shall be sent just as written. (See Chapter IV concerning charging for abbreviations, punctuation marks, etc.)

240. At the option of the sender a message need contain no text. For information as to the language which is admissible in the text see Chapter IV.

241. When a radiogram to be transmitted contains more than 40 words, the sending station shall interrupt the transmission by the signal . . — — . . after each series of about 20 words, and shall not resume it until after it has obtained from the receiving station a repetition of the last word duly received, followed by the "go ahead" signal; or, if reception is good, simply the signal — . —

242. In the case of transmission by series, acknowledgment of receipt shall be made after each radiogram.

SIGNATURE.

243. The signature follows the text but is separated therefrom by the break. At the option of the sender there may be no signature to a message, but the name and address of the sender should be taken and recorded for the purpose of forwarding notice of non-delivery, if such is received, as well as for use in making out receipt for money taken. The indication "Sig" is *not* sent before the signature

END OF MESSAGE.

244. The message is terminated by the END OF MESSAGE signal

. — . — .

followed by the name of the sending station and by the signal

— . —

245. In the case of a series of radiograms, the name of the sending station and the signal — . — shall be given only at the end of the series; at the end of each of the other messages, the sending station shall send . — . — . only, and await acknowledgment before transmitting the next message.

246. Examples of messages are given below.

(1) Ship KMO sending to NAR a plain commercial message filed on board at 4 p. m., of the 12th, after receiving "K" — . —

— . — . —
RADIO
New Orleans..............Office of destination.
De
Kingwilliam..............Office of origin.
2........................Number of message.
L........................Operator's sign.
8........................Check.
Twelfth 4pm..............Date and hour of filing on board.
— . . . — ....Break or double dash.
Brown 175 King Street
New Orleans..............Address.
— . . . — ....Break.
Arrive tomorrow..........Text.
— . . . — ....Break.
Jones....................Signature.
. — . — .
KMO
— . —

(2) Ship KRS sending to NAP a reply prepaid message to Omaha, Neb.:

— . — . —
RADIO
Omaha
De
Admiral Farragut
3
NP
12
Twelfth 4pm
— . . . —
RP one dollar eighty.......Supplementary instructions.
— . . . —
RP one dollar eighty Sherman Omaha Neb......Registered address and designation of RP message.
— . . . —
Can you meet me New Orleans Monday tenth...Text.
— . . . —
Wilson
. — . — .
KRS
— . —

(3) Paid service message relating to message in example (1). Sender desires to correct the address. From ship KMO to NAR:

— . — . —
RADIO ST................Prefix.
Keywest
De
Kingwilliam
5
XY
7
— . . . —
2 twelfth Brown...........Number, date, and address of message referred to.
Read 179 instead of 175
. — . — .
KMO
— . —

(4) LOUISIANA relaying a commercial message sent via NAR to ship *Cronstadt.* (Note.—See paragraphs 275–280 concerning relaying messages addressed to ships at sea.)

— . — . —
RADIO
Cronstadt
De
Newyork
1
H
10
Via NAR
— . . . —
Kosciusko Cronstadt Keywest
— . . . —
Herminho inexcorum koemelk pennando cobalt galibando
— . . . —
Vassily
. — . — .
NJB
— . —

ACKNOWLEDGING OR "RECEIVED" SIGNAL.

247. To acknowledge a single message or series of messages send:

(1) The call letters of the station which sent the message.

(2) The received signal . — .

(3) The number of message, or numbers of first and last messages of a series.

(4) The call letters of the receiving (i. e., acknowledging) station.

(5) Receiving operator's sign.

(6) { — . — if ready to receive another message.
— . — . — if ready to send a message.
. — . — . if you wish the other station to make "acknowledgment" only, and then listen in for you to send further.

248. Note that a sending station stops to get acknowledgment of receipt after each message, but does not send its own call letters and "K" until after the last message of the series. This distinction enables the receiving station to know whether it may proceed with its own messages or send "K" and continue to listen for further transmission.

249. The signal — . — (K) has the meaning, "I am closing off from sending to receive you." Its use by the acknowledging operator, therefore, indicates that he has nothing to send, but is prepared to receive anything further which the sending station has to transmit. Should the acknowledging station have something to transmit, the operator signals — . — . — (Attention), and begins his preamble.

250. In acknowledging each message of a series, other than the last, any station shall send simply . — . followed by the message number.

251. When the station which made the original call has received acknowledgment of what it sent, and has received and acknowledged anything the other station had for it, it shall make the "finished" signal . . . — . — followed by its call letters. The other station shall likewise make . . . — . — followed by its call letters, and the communication is thereby completed.

252. Examples of acknowledgments are given below.

(1) NMO
. — .
1
NAM
SF
— . —

(2) NAR
. — .
1
4
NWQ
EM
— . — . —
etc.

(3) NFR to NWQ acknowledging one of a series of messages.
. — .
8

CODE.

253. The signals to be employed are those of the Morse International Code. This precludes the employment of the "American Morse" for radio use by vessels licensed by the United States. The international code has likewise been adopted for use by naval vessels of the United States. Operators shall report, via official channels, to the zone officer, all infractions of this law which come to their notice. Army radio operators are required to be familiar with "American Morse," so as to be able to operate instruments on land lines when detailed to radio shore stations which are connected to land lines.

254. Operators must be familiar with the different signals used to represent characters in European languages, so as to be able to transmit and receive messages in those languages. (See Appendix I.)

255. They must also be familiar with the special numeral signals given below for use in preambles, as these are generally used by European operators in place of the larger signals of the regular code, *but these special numeral signals shall not be used by the U. S. Army Radio Service.*

INTERNATIONAL MORSE CODE SIGNALS.

LETTERS.

A	· —	J	· — — —	S	· · ·
B	— · · ·	K	— · —	T	—
C	— · — ·	L	· — · ·	U	· · —
D	— · ·	M	— —	V	· · · —
E	·	N	— ·	W	· — —
F	· · — ·	O	— — —	X	— · · —
G	— — ·	P	· — — ·	Y	— · — —
H	· · · ·	Q	— — · —	Z	— — · ·
I	· ·	R	· — ·		

NUMERALS.

1	· — — — —	6	— · · · ·
2	· · — — —	7	— — · · ·
3	· · · — —	8	— — — · ·
4	· · · · —	9	— — — — ·
5	· · · · ·	0	— — — — —

PUNCTUATION AND OTHER SIGNS.

Full stop	(.)	· · · · · ·
Semicolon	(;)	— · — · — ·
Comma	(,)	· — · — · —
Colon	(:)	— — — · · ·
Interrogation or REPEAT	(?)	· · — — · ·
Exclamation	(!)	— — · · — —
Apostrophe	(')	· — — — — ·
Hyphen or dash	(-)	— · · · · —
Bar indicating fraction	(/)	— · · — ·

Parenthesis (before and after words)	( )	— . — — . —
Quotation marks (before and after each word or each passage quoted)	(" ")	. — . . — .
Underline (before and after words or part of phrase)	(—)	. . — — . —
ATTENTION (or call)		— . — . —
Double dash or BREAK (signal separating preamble from address, address from text, and text from signature)	(=)	— . . . —
UNDERSTOOD		. . . — .
ERROR		. . . .
GO AHEAD		— . —
CROSS OR END OF MESSAGE		. — . — .
WAIT		. — . . .
RECEIVED (acknowledgment of receipt of message)		. — .
FINISHED (end of work)		. . . — . —

SPECIAL NUMERALS.

Used by European stations in the preamble of radiograms, also in the text of radiograms containing numerals only, in which case the words "in figures" are added as the last item of the preamble.

Not to be used by the U. S. Army Radio Service.

1	. —	6	— . . . .
2	. . —	7	— . . .
3	. . . —	8	— . .
4	. . . . —	9	— .
5	. . . . .	0	—

ERRORS.

256. A sending operator shall indicate an error by sending eight dots followed by the word before that sent incorrectly or before a word omitted.

EXAMPLE.

"Arrive ten to-night, stay in waters indefinite

. . . .

in these waters indefinite."

REPEATING.

257. In addition to its uses as an interrogation, the signal

. . — — . .

shall be known as the REPEAT signal, and shall be used to obtain a repetition of messages or words as follows:

(1) To have a *single message entirely repeated* send (a), call of station sending message; (b), the REPEAT signal three times; (c), station call.

(2) To have *one of a series of messages repeated* send (a), call of station sending message; (b), number of message; (c), the REPEAT signal three times; (d), station call.

(3) In case the first part of the message is received satisfactorily, indicate the last word received and get *a repetition of the last part of the message* by sending (a), call of station sending message; (b), number of message, if necessary; (c), last word received; (d), REPEAT signal; (e), station call. This will be taken to mean "Repeat after ———."

(4) In case the last part of the message was received satisfactorily, indicate the first word of the part received and *get a repetition of the message as far as that word* by sending (a), call of station sending message; (b), number of message, if necessary; (c), the REPEAT signal; (d), the first word of part received; (e), station call. This will be taken to mean "Repeat as far as ———."

(5) To *get a repetition of one or more lost or doubtful words* send (a), call of station sending message; (b), number of message, if necessary; (c), word received just before lost or doubtful word or words; (d), the REPEAT signal; (e), word after lost or doubtful words; (f), station call. This will be taken to mean "Repeat all between ——— and ———."

EXAMPLES.

(1) NAC

. . — — . .

. . — — . .

. . — — . .

NAB

— . —

(2) NAM

6

. . — — . .

. . — — . .

. . — — . .

NAL

— . —

(Repeat your No. 6)

(3) NPC

1

Report.

. . — — . .

NPD

— . —

(Repeat after word "Report.")

(4) NPO

. . — — . .

Nicholson.

NPT

— . —

(Repeat as far as "Nicholson.")

(5) NLC

4

Several.

. . — — . .

Instruct.

NAO.

— . —

PROCEDURE WHEN SIGNALS ARE DOUBTFUL.

258. When the signals become doubtful every possible means shall be resorted to to finish the transmission. To this end the radiogram shall be transmitted three times at most *at the request of the receiving station.* If, in spite of such triple repetition, the signals are still unreadable, the radiogram shall be canceled.

259. If no acknowledgment of receipt is received the transmitting station shall again call up the receiving station. If no reply is made after three calls the transmission shall not be followed up any further. In such case the sending station shall have the privilege of obtaining the acknowledgment of receipt through the medium of another radio station.

260. If, in the opinion of the receiving station, the radiogram, although imperfectly received, is nevertheless capable of transmission, said station shall enter the words "reception doubtful" at the end of the preamble and the radiogram.

SPECIAL SIGNALS.

261. The list of special signals here given is that authorized for use by the London convention. Whenever they serve the purpose they shall be used in all communication with radio stations, coast or ship, whatsoever, as the operators of all countries signatory to the convention are required to be familiar with them; they form complete messages in themselves, and do not need to be embodied in service messages.

262. When it is desired to use these signals in their interrogatory sense they must be followed by interrogation (. . — — . .).

— . — . — — . — (CQ)	Signal of *inquiry*, or general call, made by a station desiring to communicate.
— . — . (TR)	Signal preceding position report; or "Send position report."
— — . . — — (!)	Signal indicating that a station is about to send at high power.

Abbreviation.	Question.	Answer or notice.
PRB	Do you wish to communicate by means of the International Signal Code?	I wish to communicate by means of the International Signal Code.
QRA	What ship or coast station is that?	This is....
QRB	What is your distance?	My distance is....
QRC	What is your true bearing?	My true bearing is....degrees.
QRD	Where are you bound for?	I am bound for....
QRF	Where are you bound from?	I am bound from....
QRG	What line do you belong to?	I belong to the....line.
QRH	What is your wave length in meters?	My wave length is .... meters.
QRJ	How many words have you to send?	I have .... words to send.
QRK	How do you receive me?	I am receiving well.
QRL	Are you receiving badly? Shall I send 20 • • • — • for adjustment?	I am receiving badly. Please send 20 • • • — • for adjustment.
QRM	Are you being interfered with?	I am being interferred with.
QRN	Have you much static?	There is much static.
QRO	Shall I increase power?	Increase power.
QRP	Shall I decrease power?	Decrease power.
QRQ	Shall I send faster?	Send faster.
QRS	Shall I send slower?	Send slower.
QRT	Shall I stop sending?	Stop sending.
QRU	Have you anything for me?	I have nothing for you.
QRV	Are you ready?	I am ready. All right now.
QRW	Are you busy?	I am busy (or: I am busy with ....). Please do not interfere.
QRX	Shall I stand by?	Stand by. I will call you when required.
QRY	When will be my turn?	Your turn will be No. ....
QRZ	Are my signals weak?	Your signals are weak.
QSA	Are my signals strong?	Your signals are strong.
QSB	Is my tone bad? Is my spark bad?	Your tone is bad. Your spark is bad.
QSC	Is my spacing bad?	Your spacing is bad.
QSD	What is your time?	My time is ....
QSF	Is transmission to be in alternate order or in series?	Transmission will be in alternate order.
QSG	....	Transmission will be in series of 5 messages.
QSH	....	Transmission will be in series of 10 messages.
QSJ	What rate shall I collect for ....?	Collect .... for ....
QSK	Is the last radiogram canceled?	The last radiogram is canceled.
QSL	Did you get my receipt?	Please acknowledge.
QSM	What is your true course?	My true course is .... degrees.
QSN	Are you in communication with land?	I am not in communication with land.
QSO	Are you in communication with any ship or station (or, with ....)?	I am in communication with .... (through..).
QSP	Shall I inform .... that you are calling him?	Inform .... that I am calling him.
QSQ	Is .... calling me?	You are being called by ....
QSR	Will you forward the radiogram?	I will forward the radiogram.
QST	Have you received the general call?	General call to all stations.
QSU	Please call me when you have finished (or) at ... o'clock.	Will call when I have finished.
QSV	Is public correspondence [1] being handled?	Public correspondence [1] is being handled. Please do not interfere.
QSW	Shall I increase my spark frequency?	Increase your spark frequency.
QSY	Shall I send on a wave length of ... meters? ..	Let us change to the wave length of ... meters.
QSX	Shall I decrease my spark frequency?	Decrease your spark frequency.
QSZ	....	Send each word twice. I have difficulty in receiving you.
QTA		Send each radiogram twice; I have difficulty in receiving you— (or) Repeat last radiogram, reception doubtful.

[1] Public correspondence is any radio work handled on the commercial tunes 300 or 600.

When an abbreviation is followed by a mark of interrogation, it refers to the question indicated for that abbreviation.

EXAMPLES.

Station A. QRA?.............What is the name of your ship or station?

Station B. QRA *Celtic* MLC...This is the *Celtic*. Her call is MLC.

Station A. QRG?.............To what line do you belong?

Station B. QRG *White Star*....I belong to the *White Star* line.
QRZ..............Your signals are weak.

Station A then increases the power of its transmitter and sends:

Station A. QRK?............How are you receiving?
Station B. QRK..............I am receiving well.
QRB 80...........My distance is 80 nautical miles.
QRC 62...........My true bearing is 62 degrees, etc.

263. No special signals or abbreviations other than those herein authorized or those customary in the service shall be used. This prohibition extends to the special abbreviations in use among land-line operators.

INTERCEPTED MESSAGES.

264. Coast stations and ships acting singly should record (in a rough log or in a journal), with the time, all radio calls heard. They may also record the contents of any official or general messages as may be required by the officer who controls the station.

265. The contents of no private message shall, however, be copied for record by any but the station to which such a message is addressed. By private message is meant one of class D, class E, or class F. Should such a message be copied by any operator for practice in receiving, the copy must be destroyed forthwith and the contents must not be revealed.

INVIOLABILITY OF MESSAGES.

266. Operators and other authorized persons concerned with handling commercial messages are warned that the law (Appendix IV) recognizes the inviolability of private messages sent by radio as well as by telegraph, and provides penalties for divulging such messages to any but the proper persons. Operators shall exercise great care not to disclose the contents of any private message that they may handle to anyone who is not directly concerned with the reception or forwarding of such message, nor to permit any copy of such message to pass into any but the authorized channels. Operators shall not copy the contents of a private radiogram which is not addressed to their station, though it is proper that entry be made in the log of any call or communication overheard, and desirable that such entries be made at stations where radio traffic is not heavy, as they frequently are of service in tracing reports of failure to communicate, etc.

FORWARDING RADIOGRAMS BY RADIO.

(*a*) MESSAGES FOR SHIPS.

267. A message received by a coast station for transmission to a ship shall be transmitted to the ship addressed as soon as practicable after she comes within range.

268. If the ship for which a radiogram is intended has not signaled her presence to the coast station within the period designated by the sender, or, in the absence of such designation, by the morning of the eighth day following, the coast station shall so notify the office of origin, which shall in turn inform the sender.

269. The latter shall have the right to ask, by a paid service message sent by either telegraph or mail, and addressed to the coast station, that his radiogram be held for a further period of nine days for transmission to the vessel, and so on. In the absence of such request, the radiogram shall be put aside as not transmissible, at the end of the ninth day (exclusive of the day of filing).

270. Nevertheless, if the coast station is certain that the vessel has left its radius of action before it has been able to transmit the radiogram to her, such station shall immediately so notify the office of origin, which shall without delay inform the sender of the cancellation of the message. The sender may, however, by a paid service message, request the coast station to transmit the radiogram the next time the vessel shall pass.

271. This section is important. In the past some operators have wrongly serviced back nondelivery immediately upon receipt of a message, because the ship was not, at that time, in range. *This is to be done only in case that it is known that the ship has already passed.*

(*b*) MESSAGES FROM SHIPS.

272. In general, ships shall transmit their radiograms to the *nearest* coast station open to commercial business.

A sender on board a vessel shall, however, have the right to designate the coast station through which he desires to have his radiogram transmitted. The ship shall then wait until such coast station shall be the nearest.

273. In exceptional cases transmission may be made to a more distant coast station, provided that:

(a) The radiogram is intended for the country in which such coast station is situated and emanates from a ship subject to that country.

(b) Both stations use for calling and transmission a wave length of 1,800 meters.

(c) Transmission with this wave length does not interfere with a transmission made by means of the same wave length by a nearer coast station.

(d) The station on shipboard is more than 50 nautical miles distant from any coast station open to commercial business. The distance of 50 miles may be reduced to 25 miles, provided the maximum power at the terminals of the generator does not exceed 5 k. w.

274. Operators will note that this permission to communicate with other than the nearest station is very much restricted. Foreign vessels on the coast of the United States have no right to do so, nor has any ship the right, when, by so doing, it interferes with business of a nearer station. Operators shall report to the zone officer all violations of this section coming under their notice.

RELAYING BY RADIO.

275. Relaying of messages by radio is now authorized and mandatory under certain conditions. Therefore, whenever these conditions prevail, a coast station or ship shall relay commercial messages.

276. Messages are entitled to be relayed under the following conditions:

In case direct communication can not be established between the stations of origin and destination.

In case the relaying is solely for the purpose of reaching the nearest coast station (if message originates from a ship).

In case the relaying ship or station is in position to forward the message.

In case the total number of relays does not exceed two.

277. Messages originating on a ship may be relayed to another ship by means of one or two ships, by means of a coast station, or by means of two coast stations and their connecting telegraph lines. Messages from shore may be relayed to a ship by other ships, *but only in case the sender has specifically demanded such relay,* in which case the preamble contains the instruction "x retransmissions," "x" standing for the number of relays authorized (not exceeding two); or this information may come by service message. In these cases the coast station forwards the message by one or two relay ships and then notifies the office of origin what the amount of relay charges is so that they may be collected of the sender.

278. The regular ship or station charge is by international convention permitted to be made for relaying messages, there being but one charge for relaying (*i. e.*, the reception and retransmission is made a single, not a double charge). All relay charges must be prepaid, as must all other charges on radiograms. The United States Army, also the Naval Radio Service, makes no charge for relaying radiograms, nor do certain of the commercial companies. The latter includes the Marconi Wireless Telegraph Co. and affiliated companies. (See par. 86.)

279. Relayed messages shall be reported the same as messages which are originated or received, but no charge shall be entered.

280. Except in Alaska, relaying between coast stations is prohibited, except in very unusual circumstances, when land lines are down and messages are of urgent nature. Alaskan stations relay to one another as necessary to forward messages to destinations.

FORWARDING COMMERCIAL MESSAGES OVER LAND LINES.

281. Coast stations shall, for the purpose of handling messages and the accounts relating thereto, consider the local telegraph office, or offices, the same as a ship or radio station.

281a. They shall maintain a daily series of numbers on messages sent to a telegraph office, giving each message its consecutive number in the preamble, the same as though it were to be transmitted by radio.

282. The preamble shall show the word RADIO, in all cases, to indicate that the message is a radiogram. It shall show as office of origin the *name* (not call letters) of the ship from which it originated, followed by the *name* of the coast station.

283. It shall not bear the date and hour of filing on board ship, but the operator or clerk shall note in his records the date and hour the message is turned over to the telegraph office.

284. If any route has been designated by the sender of the message, such route shall be written at the end of the address. Use "P" for Postal and "W" for Western Union. Cable lines shall be designated by the common abbreviations used commercially.

285. If any supplementary instructions were received, as, for example, those designating a special class of radiogram, they shall be written in an abbreviated form just before the address and count as one word in the check.

286. The address, text, and signature shall be written exactly as received.

287. Those stations which have connection to both Postal and Western Union lines shall divide their business between the two companies. When an answer is received by radio to a message which was forwarded through the coast station it should be sent over the same line as that from which the original message was received. If a coast station receives a message addressed to a place which may be reached by more than one route, and no route has been designated by the sender, the coast station shall forward it by the most direct or cheapest route, if there be any difference in rates.

288. The check must be entered as received. If there is any discrepancy therein, it should have been adjusted with the operator from whom received. In case of disagreement which can not be reconciled note shall be made thereof on the copy message which is sent to the zone officer.

MESSAGES ACCEPTED DIRECT FROM THE SENDER.

289. All messages offered by the public at coast stations open to public business shall be received by the electrician in charge, as far as practicable. Should a message be offered for transmission to a ship at sea through another coast station, the sender should be referred to the nearest land-wire office. On board ship messages are received by the chief radio operator or other properly designated person. Should a message be offered to a coast station not open to public business, the sender shall be referred to the nearest commercial station.

BLANK.

290. A message filed at a radio station shall be legibly written or typewritten on a radio message form, or attached to the form by the sender, or the person presenting the message as the sender's agent.

291. The sender should write, first, the route (if he wishes to specify any); second, the special instructions, if any (that is, for a radiogram of special class; see Chapter III); third, the address; fourth, the text; fifth, the signature. Neither text nor signature is obligatory, however.

TIMING OF MESSAGES, ETC.

292. Each message shall be timed by the operator or clerk receiving it, who shall see that the month and day are correctly noted thereon (the time and day are transmitted in case of a ship-to-shore message); he shall also carefully read the message before accepting it, and, when necessary, shall make it plain by marginal notation.

293. The receiving operator or clerk shall courteously and patiently give all information requested and shall assist the sender in every way practicable in formulating the address, etc., in order that errors or delays may be avoided. Attention shall be called to misspelled words and combinations contrary to the usage of the language in plain language messages, and all unnecessary punctuation marks, etc.; but everything written by the sender on the blank shall be transmitted if he so requests.

ADDRESS AND SIGNATURE.

294. The importance of the address can not be overestimated. In the case of a surname only being offered as an address, the possibility of several persons of the same name being aboard the ship to which the message is addressed should be pointed out to the sender. Addresses of messages for shore must contain sufficient information to enable the addressee to be located. Except in case of a registered address, the street and number should be given (as well as town), unless the town is very small.

295. A message for a ship handed in at a coast station need have only the name of the person and the name of the ship. The latter, in all cases, shall be counted as one word. The address of a message originating on shore, not at a coast station, must contain (a) name of addressee, (b) name of ship, (c) name of coast station through which it is to be sent.

296. When a message is offered without signature, the sender's attention should be called to the omission; also to the fact that no signature is required except as information which might be necessary to the addressee.

CHARGES.

297. The charges to be collected shall be determined by the operator in charge from the tables given in Chapter II. The charge comprises (a) the coast station rate, (b) the ship rate, (c) the land-line or cable rate, (d) the ship rate for each ship relaying, where such transmission is involved, except for such systems as make no charge for relaying (see par. 278). As many schedules of rates as are available are included in Chapter II. If the rates desired are not given there, they may be obtained by service messages, if practicable; otherwise, a charge of 8 cents for ship rate shall be assumed and 12 cents for coast station rate. In case of a commercial message sent from ship to ship, the charge consists of the ship charge for each ship, prepaid, except as prescribed in paragraph 63.

RECEIPT.

298. The receiving operator shall make out a receipt in duplicate (Form 150) for the amount collected in cash, and shall sign both copies. One copy shall be attached to the back of the message blank and the other shall be given to the sender. Should the sender decline to take the receipt, it shall be attached to the message, marked "Refused."

ADDRESS OF SENDER.

299. On the receipt the address of the sender shall be placed after his name. If the address is temporary, a second address at which the sender may receive mail should be requested.

UNDELIVERED RADIOGRAMS FROM SHIPS.

300. When, for any reason, a message from a ship at sea can not be delivered to the addressee, the coast station will be informed, by service message, by the telegraph office of destination; the operator at the coast station shall then compare the address given in the service message with that in his file copy of the original, and, if necessary, correct it. If there is no discrepancy he shall forward the service message, if possible, to the ship on which the message originated, through the intervention, if need be, of another coast station. The ship operator should then compare the address on the original message in his files with that given in the notice of non-delivery, and shall send a correcting service message if he finds any discrepancy. In the absence of any discrepancy he shall inform the sender of the nondelivery of the message and of the reason assigned for it. Should the sender desire to add to or alter the address he may do so by *paid service message*. Some of the reasons for nondelivery of a message may be:

Addressee unknown.
Addressee left.
Addressee deceased.
Addressee not arrived.
Addressee not registered.
Addressee no longer registered.
Address unknown.
Refused.

UNDELIVERED RADIOGRAMS ON BOARD SHIP.

301. When a message reaching a ship at sea can not be delivered, the office of origin should be informed by a service message. This information should be sent, if possible, through the coast station from which the message was received; but if circumstances require, it may be sent through the nearest coast station. Reasons for nondelivery on board ship may be:

Addressee not on board.
Addressee no longer on board.
Addressee unknown.
Addressee deceased.
Refused.

APPENDIX I.

NOTES ON VARIATIONS IN FORMS USED BY FOREIGN STATIONS.

The following brief notes cover some of the points of difference in form and abbreviations used by radio stations of other countries. They are *not* to be used by U. S. army operators, but are here inserted merely for convenience, and as an aid in helping operators interpret signals which may be sent to them by foreign stations or ships.

European stations transmit the word "Radio" in the preamble of *all* messages, whether official, commercial, service, or otherwise. The British order of transmission is:

Prefix.
"Radio."
Name of ship or office of origin.
No. of message.
Check.
Date and hour of filing.
Route (if any).
Supplementary instructions (special classes, etc.).

No prefix is used for a plain commercial message, the word "Radio" sufficing. The prefixes used for various other classes are:

"S"—Government message.
"A"—Service message.
"ST"—Paid service message.
"Presse"—Press message.
"D"—Urgent message.
"B"—Indicates that the sending station is the office of origin and the receiving station the office of destination.

It must be remembered that many European stations use the special numerals (abbreviated form) in the preamble of all messages.

The date and hour of filing are expressed by two groups of figures, the first representing the month, the second the hour and minutes, followed by "m" for a. m., and "s" for p. m. Thus:

2:30 p. m., of the 12th=12 2:30 s.

European ships use "D" as prefix for urgent messages. These can not be accepted in the United States, and a service message to that effect should be sent to the ship if such a message is received.

In acknowledging receipt of a series of messages, some European ships signal (after "R" . — .), first, the total number of messages received, then the numbers of the first and last messages of the series.

The international convention stipulates that service communications between stations of different nationalities shall be made in French. There is, therefore, given below a list of the more usual French experessions so employed for the use of operators who may receive a service message in that language:

English.	French.
Sender	Expéditeur
Addressee	Destinataire
Unknown	Inconnu
Left	Parti
Not on board	Pas à bord
No longer on board	Plus à bord

English.	French.
Deceased	Décédé
Address	Addressee
Not registered	Pas enregistrée
No longer registered	Plus enregistrée
Refused	Refusé
For	Pour
With	Avec
From	De
To	A
Repeat	Répétons
Already	Déjà
Delivered	Remis
Deliver	Remettez
Cancel	Annulez
Replace	Remplacez
Read (*e. g.*, "for *nine* read *nineteen*")	Lisez
See	Voyez
Reply paid	Réponse payée
Radiogram to be repeated	Collationnement
Mailed as a registered letter	Poste recommandée
Prepaid special delivery	Exprès payé
Our	Notre
Your	Votre
Radiogram	Radiotélégramme
Telegraphic acknowledgment of receipt (PC)	Accusé réception télégraphique
Postal acknowledgment of receipt (PCP)	Accusé réception postale
Mail	Poste
Registered mail	Poste recommandée
Special delivery	Exprès
Prepaid	Payé
Day	Jour
Night	Nuit
A. M.	Matin (abbreviation "m")
P. M.	Soir (abbreviation "s")
Name	Nom
City	Ville
Country	Pays
Care of	Chez
Office	Bureau
Call letters	Indicatif d'appel
Service message	Avis
Paid service message	Service taxé
Number (*e. g.*, *number* of message or house *number*)	Numéro
Number (amount, *e. g.*, *number* of words)	Nombre
Replace..by	Remplacez..par..
Plain language	Langage clair
Code language	Langage convenu.
Cipher language	Langage chiffré
Charge	Taxe
Coast charge	Taxe côtière
Ship charge	Taxe de bord
Charge per word	Taxe par mot
Land-line charge	Taxe télégraphique

APPENDIX II.

TIME SIGNALS AND HYDROGRAPHIC INFORMATION BY RADIO.

The United States Naval Radio Service is furnishing information to vessels at sea, as follows:

TIME SIGNALS.

Time signals will be sent out broadcast by the following stations on the Atlantic and Pacific coasts of the United States:

Station.	Wave length.	When sent.
	Meters.	
Arlington	2,500	Every day at 11.55 a. m. to noon and 9.55 to 10 p. m., standard time, 75th meridian.
Key West	1,000	Daily, at 11.55 a. m. to noon, standard time, 75th meridian.
New Orleans	1,000	Same as Key West.
North Head	2,000	Daily, except Sundays and holidays, at 11.55 a. m. to noon, standard time, 120th meridian.
Eureka	1,400	Same as North Head.
San Diego	2,000	Do.
Mare Island	2,500	Every day at 11.55 a. m. to noon and 9.55 to 10 p. m., standard time, 120th meridian.

If for any reason the Arlington Station is out of commission the time signal will be sent daily at noon, Sundays and holidays excepted, by the Naval Radio Stations at Newport, New York, Norfolk, and Charleston.

The time is sent from the Naval Observatory, Washington, for the Atlantic coast, and from the observatory at the Mare Island Navy Yard for the Pacific coast.

The radio sending or relay key in each radio station is connected to the Western Union lines by a relay at about 11.50 a. m., and the signals are made automatically direct from Washington or Mare Island.

Time signals from each of the observatories mentioned continue for the five minutes preceding noon and 10 p. m. During this interval every tick of the clock is transmitted, except the 29th second of each minute, the last five seconds of each of the first four minutes, and finally the last ten seconds of the last minute. The noon (and 10 p. m.) signal is a longer contact after this longer break.

It is not necessary that an elaborate radio installation be employed for the purpose of receiving these signals, nor that a skilled operator be in attendance. Any vessel provided with a small receiving apparatus with one or two wires hoisted as high as possible and insulated from all metal fittings, or preferably stretched between the mastheads with one wire led down to the receiver, may detect these signals when within range of one of the seacoast radio stations.

These time signals have been used successfully by vessels for rating their chronometers and have been used by surveying vessels in the accurate determination of longitudes.

HYDROGRAPHIC INFORMATION.

Information concerning wrecks, derelicts, ice, and other dangerous obstructions to navigation whenever received from the Hydrographic Office or from a branch hydrographic office is sent broadcast four times daily, viz, at 8 a. m., noon, 4 p. m., and 8 p. m., local (standard) time of station. Ships within range of a naval radio station should be prepared to receive these hydrographic messages at the hours mentioned and should avoid sending radio messages at these times. One vessel sending may prevent several others receiving information necessary to their safety.

Naval radio stations will furnish this information to passing vessels on request, whenever practicable, at other hours than those mentioned above. Should it not be practicable to send out this information on one of the hours scheduled it will be held until the next scheduled time and sent out as soon as practicable after each hour scheduled.

Each night at 10 p. m., seventy-fifth meridian, immediately following the time signal, the Naval Radio Station at Arlington, Va., will broadcast such information relating to safe navigation as may be furnished it by the Hydrographic Office during the preceding 24 hours. The same wave length, 2,500 meters, used in the time signal will be employed.

APPENDIX III.

DISTRIBUTION OF METEOROLOGICAL INFORMATION BY RADIO SERVICE.

U. S. Department of Agriculture.
Central Office of the Weather Bureau,
Washington, D. C., July 1, 1913.

It is announced that beginning July 15, 1913, a weather bulletin will be distributed broadcast by the naval radio stations at Radio, Va., and Key West, Fla., a few minutes after 10 p. m. each day. *The broadcast distribution will be exclusively by the naval radio stations above named,* but all other naval radio stations will continue to distribute meteorological information and forecasts as at present.

The daily bulletin will consist of two parts. The first part will contain code letters and figures which will express the actual weather conditions at 8 p. m., seventy-fifth meridian time, on the day of distribution at certain points along the eastern coast of North America, one point along the coast of the Gulf of Mexico, and one at Bermuda. The second part of the bulletin will contain a special forecast of the probable winds to be experienced a hundred miles or so off shore, made by the United States Weather Bureau for distribution to shipmasters by naval radio as above. The second part of the bulletin will also contain *warnings of severe storms* along the coast as occasion may arise.

The points for which weather conditions will be furnished will be designated respectively by their initial letter, except in the case of Nantucket, for which the letter T will be used; accordingly, S=Sydney, T=Nantucket, A=Atlantic City, H=Hatteras, C=Charleston, K=Key West, P=Pensacola, and B=Bermuda.

The bulletin will begin with the letters U S W B for U. S. Weather Bureau, and the weather conditions will follow. The first three figures of a report will represent the barometic pressure in inches (0.02=30.02); the next figure, the fourth in sequence, will represent the direction of the wind to eight points of the compass: 1=north, 2=northeast, 3=east, 4=southeast, 5=south, 6=southwest, 7=west, 8=northwest, and 0=calm. The fifth figure will represent the force of the wind on the Beaufort scale.

Beaufort scale of wind force.

Number and designation.	Statute miles per hour.	Nautical miles per hour.
0—Calm	0 to 3	0 to 2.6
1—Light air	8	6.9
2—Light breeze	13	11.3
3—Gentle breeze	18	15.6
4—Moderate breeze	23	20.0
5—Fresh breeze	28	24.3
6—Strong breeze	34	29.5
7—Moderate gale	40	34.7
8—Fresh gale	48	41.6
9—Strong gale	56	48.6
10—Whole gale	65	56.4
11—Storm	75	65.1
12—Hurricane	[1] 90	[1] 78.1

[1] And over.

In order to simplify the code no provision has been made for wind force greater than 9, strong gale on the Beaufort scale. Whenever winds of force greater than 9 occur the number representing them will be given in words instead of figures, thus: Ten, eleven, etc.

The entire group of stations will be transmitted from Radio, Va., but the group transmitted from Key West will not for the present contain Sydney. If the weather conditions from any station can not be supplied, the initial of the station will be given followed by the word "missing," and if any portion of a report can not be furnished, such portion will be replaced by an equivalent number of letters, x.

EXAMPLE OF CODE.

U. S. W. B. S 96465 T 91674 A 94686 H 99886 C 01214 K 02622 P 03613 B 00065.

United States Weather Bureau translation.

Stations.	Pressure.	Wind.	
		Direction.	Force.
Sydney	29.64	SW.	5
Nantucket	29.16	W.	4
Atlantic City	29.46	NW.	6
Hatteras	29.98	NW.	6
Charleston	30.12	N.	4
Key West	30.26	NE.	2
Pensacola	30.36	N.	3
Bermuda	30.00	SW.	5

The second part of the bulletin will contain a wind forecast for the coastal waters of the eastern part of the United States and the Gulf States.

The coast line will be divided as follows:

North Atlantic, Halifax to New York; middle Atlantic, New York to Hatteras; south Atlantic, Hatteras to Key West; east Gulf, Key West to mouth of the Mississippi; west Gulf, mouth of Mississippi to mouth of Rio Grande.

The forecasts and warnings will be in ordinary language and will cover a period of 48 hours from time of issue. At the end of the forecasts a statement will be made in reference to the location and movement of any barometric depression that may be likely to affect the winds over the ocean.

EXAMPLE OF FORECASTS AND WARNINGS.

Winds Thursday and Friday, north Atlantic coast, brisk westerly, diminishing; middle Atlantic coast, fresh westerly becoming light and variable; south Atlantic coast, moderate and variable; east Gulf coast, light northerly becoming east to south; west Gulf coast, moderate southerly. Depression in Saint Lawrence Valley; pressure 9.46 at Quebec; moving east-northeast; storm warnings displayed Nantucket to Eastport.

APPENDIX IV.

UNITED STATES LAW GOVERNING RADIO COMMUNICATION.

[PUBLIC—No. 264.]

[S. 6412.]

AN ACT TO REGULATE RADIO COMMUNICATION.

Be it enacted by the Senate and House of Representatives of the United States of America in Congress assembled, That a person, company, or corporation within the jurisdiction of the United States shall not use or operate any apparatus for radio communication as a means of commercial intercourse among the several States, or with foreign nations, or upon any vessel of the United States engaged in interstate or foreign commerce, or for the transmission of radiograms or signals the effect of which extends beyond the jurisdiction of the State or Territory in which the same are made, or where interference would be caused thereby with the receipt of messages or signals from beyond the jurisdiction of the said State or Territory, except under and in accordance with a license, revocable for cause, in that behalf granted by the Secretary of Commerce and Labor upon application therefor; but nothing in this act shall be construed to apply to the transmission and exchange of radiograms or signals between points situated in the same State: *Provided*, That the effect thereof shall not extend beyond the jurisdiction of the said State or interfere with the reception of radiograms or signals from beyond said jurisdiction; and a license shall not be required for the transmission or exchange of radiograms or signals by or on behalf of the Government of the United States, but every Government station on land or sea shall have special call letters designated and published in the list of radio stations of the United States by the Department of Commerce and Labor. Any person, company, or corporation that shall use or operate any apparatus for radio communication in violation of this section, or knowingly aid or abet another person, company, or corporation in so doing, shall be deemed guilty of a misdemeanor, and on conviction thereof shall be punished by a fine not exceeding five hundred dollars, and the apparatus or device so unlawfully used and operated may be adjudged forfeited to the United States.

SEC. 2. That every such license shall be in such form as the Secretary of Commerce and Labor shall determine and shall contain the restrictions, pursuant to this act, on and subject to which the license is granted; that every such license shall be issued only to citizens of the United States or Porto Rico or to a company incorporated under the laws of some State or Territory or of the United States or Porto Rico, and shall specify the ownership and location of the station in which said apparatus shall be used and other particulars for its identification and to enable its range to be estimated, shall state the purpose of the station, and, in case of a station in actual operation at the date of passage of this act, shall contain the statement that satisfactory proof has been furnished that it was actually operating on the above-mentioned date; shall state the wave length or the wave lengths authorized for use by the station for the prevention of interference and the hours for which the station is licensed for work; and shall not be construed to authorize the use of any apparatus for radio communication in any other station than that specified. Every such license shall be subject to the regulations contained herein, and such regulations as may be established from time to time by authority of this act or subsequent acts and treaties of the United States. Every such license shall provide that the President of the United States in time of war or public peril or disaster may cause the closing of any station for radio communication and the removal therefrom of all radio apparatus, or may authorize the use or control of any such station or apparatus by any department of the Government, upon just compensation to the owners.

SEC. 3. That every such apparatus shall at all times while in use and operation as aforesaid be in charge or under the supervision of a person or persons licensed for that purpose by the Secretary of Commerce and Labor. Every person so licensed who in the operation of any radio apparatus shall fail to observe and obey regulations contained in or made pursuant to this act or subsequent acts or treaties of the United States, or any one of them, or who shall fail to enforce obedience thereto by an unlicensed person while serving under his supervision, in addition to the punishments and penalties herein prescribed, may suffer the suspension of the said license for a period to be fixed by the Secretary of Commerce and Labor not exceeding one year. It shall be unlawful to employ any unlicensed person or for any unlicensed person to serve in charge or in supervision of the use and operation of such apparatus, and any person violating this provision shall be guilty of a misdemeanor, and on conviction thereof shall be punished by a fine of not more than one hundred dollars or imprisonment for not more than two months, or both, in the discretion of the court, for each and every such offense: *Provided*, That in case of emergency the Secretary of Commerce and Labor may authorize a collector of customs to issue a temporary permit, in lieu of a license, to the operator on a vessel subject to the radio ship act of June twenty-fourth, nineteen hundred and ten.

SEC. 4. That for the purpose of preventing or minimizing interference with communication between stations in which such apparatus is operated, to facilitate radio communication, and to further the prompt receipt of distress signals, said private and commercial stations shall be subject to the regulations of this section. These regulations shall be enforced by the Secretary of Commerce and Labor through the collectors of customs and other officers of the Government as other regulations herein provided for.

The Secretary of Commerce and Labor may, in his discretion, waive the provisions of any or all of these regulations when no interference of the character above mentioned can ensue.

The Secretary of Commerce and Labor may grant special temporary licenses to stations actually engaged in conducting experiments for the development of the science of radio communication, or the apparatus pertaining thereto, to carry on special tests, using any amount of power or any wave lengths, at such hours and under such conditions as will insure the least interference with the sending or receipt of commercial or Government radiograms, of distress signals and radiograms, or with the work of other stations.

In these regulations the naval and military stations shall be understood to be stations on land.

REGULATIONS.

NORMAL WAVE LENGTHS.

First. Every station shall be required to designate a certain definite wave length as the normal sending and receiving wave length of the station. This wave length shall not exceed six hundred meters or it shall exceed one thousand six hundred meters. Every coastal station open to general public service shall at all times be ready to receive messages of such wave lengths as are required by the Berlin convention. Every ship station, except as hereinafter provided, and every coast station open to general public service shall be prepared to use two sending wave lengths, one of three hundred meters and one of six hundred meters, as required by the international convention in force: *Provided*, That the Secretary of Commerce and Labor may, in his discretion, change the limit of wave length reservation made by regulations first and second to accord with any international agreement to which the United States is a party.

OTHER WAVE LENGTHS.

Second. In addition to the normal sending wave length all stations, except as provided hereinafter in these regulations, may use other sending wave lengths: *Provided*, That they do not exceed six hundred meters or that they do exceed one thousand six hundred meters: *Provided further*, That the character of the waves emitted conforms to the requirements of regulations third and fourth following.

USE OF A "PURE WAVE."

Third. At all stations if the sending apparatus, to be referred to hereinafter as the "transmitter," is of such a character that the energy is radiated in two or more wave lengths, more or less sharply defined, as indicated by a sensitive wave meter, the energy in no one of the lesser waves shall exceed ten per centum of that in the greatest.

USE OF A "SHARP WAVE."

Fourth. At all stations the logarithmic decrement per complete oscillation in the wave trains emitted by the transmitter shall not exceed two-tenths, except when sending distress signals or signals and messages relating thereto.

USE OF "STANDARD DISTRESS WAVE."

Fifth. Every station on shipboard shall be prepared to send distress calls on the normal wave length designated by the international convention in force, except on vessels of small tonnage unable to have plants insuring that wave length.

SIGNAL OF DISTRESS.

Sixth. The distress call used shall be the international signal of distress—

• • • — — — • • •

USE OF "BROAD INTERFERING WAVE" FOR DISTRESS SIGNALS.

Seventh. When sending distress signals, the transmitter of a station on shipboard may be tuned in such a manner as to create a maximum of interference with a maximum of radiation.

DISTANCE REQUIREMENT FOR DISTRESS SIGNALS.

Eighth. Every station on shipboard, wherever practicable, shall be prepared to send distress signals of the character specified in regulations fifth and sixth with sufficient power to enable them to be received by day over sea a distance of one hundred nautical miles by a shipboard station equipped with apparatus for both sending and receiving equal in all essential particulars to that of the station first mentioned.

"RIGHT OF WAY" FOR DISTRESS SIGNALS.

Ninth. All stations are required to give absolute priority to signals and radiograms relating to ships in distress; to cease all sending on hearing a distress signal; and, except when engaged in answering or aiding the ship in distress, to refrain from sending until all signals and radiograms relating thereto are completed.

REDUCED POWER FOR SHIPS NEAR A GOVERNMENT STATION.

Tenth. No station on shipboard, when within fifteen nautical miles of a naval or military station, shall use a transformer input exceeding one kilowatt, nor when within five nautical miles of such station, a transformer input exceeding one-half kilowatt, except for sending signals of distress, or signals or radiograms relating thereto.

INTERCOMMUNICATION.

Eleventh. Each shore station open to general public service between the coast and vessels at sea shall be bound to exchange radio grams with any similar shore station and with any ship station without distinction of the radio systems adopted by such stations, respectively, and each station on shipboard shall be bound to exchange radiograms with any other station on shipboard without distinction of the radio systems adopted by each station, respectively.

It shall be the duty of each such shore station, during the hours it is in operation, to listen in at intervals of not less than fifteen minutes and for a period not less than two minutes, with the receiver tuned to receive messages of three hundred-meter wave length.

DIVISION OF TIME.

Twelfth. At important seaports and at all other places where naval or military and private or commercial shore stations operate in such close proximity that interference with the work of naval and military stations can not be avoided by the enforcement of the regulations contained in the foregoing regulations concerning wave lengths and character of signals emitted, such private or commercial shore stations as do interfere with the reception of signals by the naval and military stations concerned shall not use their transmitters during the first fifteen minutes of each hour, local standard time. The Secretary of Commerce and Labor may, on the recommendation of the department concerned, designate the station or stations which may be required to observe this division of time.

GOVERNMENT STATIONS TO OBSERVE DIVISION OF TIME.

Thirteenth. The naval or military stations for which the above-mentioned division of time may be established shall transmit signals or radiograms only during the first fifteen minutes of each hour, local standard time, except in case of signals or radiograms relating to vessels in distress, as hereinbefore provided.

USE OF UNNECESSARY POWER.

Fourteenth. In all circumstances, except in case of signals or radiograms relating to vessels in distress, all station shall use the minimum amount of energy necessary to carry out any communication desired.

GENERAL RESTRICTIONS ON PRIVATE STATIONS.

Fifteenth. No private or commercial station not engaged in the transaction of bona fide commercial business by radio communication or in experimentation in connection with the development and manufacture of radio apparatus for commercial purposes shall use a transmitting wave length exceeding two hundred meters, or a transformer input exceeding one kilowatt, except by special authority of the Secretary of Commerce and Labor contained in the license of the station: *Provided*, That the owner or operator of a station of the character mentioned in this regulation shall not be liable for a violation of the requirements of the third or fourth regulations to the penalties of one hundred dollars or twenty-five dollars, respectively, provided in this section unless the person maintaining or operating such station shall have been notified in writing that the said transmitter has been found, upon tests conducted by the Government, to be so adjusted as to violate the said third and fourth regulations, and opportunity has been given to said owner or operator to adjust said transmitter in conformity with said regulations.

SPECIAL RESTRICTIONS IN THE VICINITIES OF GOVERNMENT STATIONS.

Sixteenth. No station of the character mentioned in regulation fifteenth situated within five nautical miles of a naval or military station shall use a transmitting wave length exceeding two hundred meters or a transformer input exceeding one-half kilowatt.

SHIP STATIONS TO COMMUNICATE WITH NEAREST SHORE STATIONS.

Seventeenth. In general, the shipboard stations shall transmit their radiograms to the nearest shore station. A sender on board a vessel shall, however, have the right to designate the shore station through which he desires to have his radiograms transmitted. If this can not be done, the wishes of the sender are to be complied with only if the transmission can be effected without interfering with the service of other stations.

LIMITATIONS FOR FUTURE INSTALLATIONS IN VICINITIES OF GOVERNMENT STATIONS.

Eighteenth. No station on shore not in actual operation at the date of the passage of this act shall be licensed for the transaction of commercial business by radio communication within 15 nautical miles of the following naval or military stations, to wit: Arlington, Virginia; Key West, Florida; San Juan, Porto Rico; North Head and Tatoosh Island, Washington; San Diego, California; and those established or which may be established in Alaska and in the Canal Zone; and the head of the department having control of such Government stations shall, so far as is consistent with the transaction of governmental business, arrange for the transmission and receipt of commercial radiograms under the provisions of the Berlin convention of nineteen hundred and six and future international conventions or treaties to which the United States may be a party, at each of the stations above referred to, and shall fix the rates therefor, subject to control of such rates by Congress. At such stations and wherever and whenever shore stations open for general public business between the coast and vessels at sea under the provisions of the Berlin convention of nineteen hundred and six and future international conventions and treaties to which the United States may be a party shall not be so established as to insure a constant service day and night without interruption, and in all localities wherever or whenever such service shall not be maintained by a commercial shore station within one hundred nautical miles of a naval radio station, the Secretary of the Navy shall, so far as is consistent with the transaction of governmental business, open naval radio stations to the general public business described above, and shall fix rates for such service, subject to control of such rates by Congress. The receipts from such radiograms shall be covered into the Treasury as miscellaneous receipts.

SECRECY OF MESSAGES.

Nineteenth. No person or persons engaged in or having knowledge of the operation of any station or stations, shall divulge or publish the contents of any messages transmitted or received by such station, except to the person or persons to whom the same may be directed, or their authorized agent, or to another station employed to forward such message to its destination, unless legally required so to do by the court of competent jurisdiction or other competent authority. Any person guilty of divulging or publishing any message, except as herein provided, shall, on conviction thereof, be punishable by a fine of not more than two hundred and fifty dollars or imprisonment for a period of not exceeding three months, or both fine and imprisonment, in the discretion of the court.

PENALTIES.

For violation of any of these regulations, subject to which a license under sections one and two of this act may be issued, the owner of the apparatus shall be liable to a penalty of one hundred dollars, which may be reduced or remitted by the Secretary of Commerce and Labor, and for repeated violations of any of such regulations the license may be revoked.

For violation of any of these regulations, except as provided in regulation nineteenth, subject to which a license under section three of this act may be issued, the operator shall be subject to a penalty of twenty-five dollars, which may be reduced or remitted by the Secretary of Commerce and Labor, and for repeated violations of any such regulations, the license shall be suspended or revoked.

SEC. 5. That every license granted under the provisions of this act for the operation or use of apparatus for radio communication shall prescribe that the operator thereof shall not willfully or maliciously interfere with any radio communication. Such interference shall be deemed a misdemeanor, and upon conviction thereof the owner or operator, or both, shall be punishable by a fine of not to exceed five hundred dollars or imprisonment for not to exceed one year, or both.

SEC. 6. That the expression "radio communication" as used in this act means any system of electrical communication by telegraphy or telephony without the aid of any wire connecting the points from and at which the radiograms, signals, or other communications are sent or received.

SEC. 7. That a person, company, or corporation within the jurisdiction of the United States shall not knowingly utter or transmit, or cause to be uttered or transmitted, any false or fraudulent distress signal or call or false or fraudulent signal, call, or other radiogram of any kind. The penalty for so uttering or transmitting a false or fraudulent distress signal or call shall be a fine of not more than two thousand five hundred dollars or imprisonment for not more than five years, or both, in the discretion of the court, for each and every such offense, and the penalty for so uttering or transmitting, or causing to be uttered or transmitted any other false or fraudulent signal, call, or other radiogram shall be a fine of not more than one thousand dollars or imprisonment for not more than two years, or both, in the discretion of the court, for each and every such offense.

SEC. 8. That a person, company, or corporation shall not use or operate any apparatus for radio communication on a foreign ship in territorial waters of the United States otherwise than in accordance with the provisions of sections four and seven of this act and so much of section five as imposes a penalty for interference. Save as aforesaid, nothing in this act shall apply to apparatus for radio communication on any foreign ship.

SEC. 9. That the trial of any offense under this act shall be in the district in which it is committed, or if the offense is committed upon the high seas or out of the jurisdiction of any particular State or district the trial shall be in the district where the offender may be found or into which he shall be first brought.

SEC. 10. That this act shall not apply to the Philippine Islands.

SEC. 11. That this act shall take effect and be in force on and after four months from its passage.

Approved, August 13, 1912.

APPENDIX V.

A PROCLAMATION.

BY THE PRESIDENT OF THE UNITED STATES OF AMERICA.

Whereas a radiotelegraphic convention, with the final protocol and service regulations, between the United States and other Governments was concluded and signed by their respective plenipotentiaries at London on the fifth day of July, one thousand nine hundred and twelve, the originals of which convention, final protocol and service regulations, being in the French language, are word for word as follows:

[Here follow the text of the convention and signatures of the delegates, certified correct by the British under secretary for foreign affairs.]

And whereas the said convention has been duly ratified by the Government of the United States of America, by and with the advice and consent of the Senate thereof, and by Belgium (and the Belgian Kongo), Denmark, Egypt, Germany, Great Britain, Italy, Monaco, Netherlands, the Netherlands Indies and the Colony of Curaçao, Roumania, Russia, Siam, and Spain, and the ratifications of the said Governments were, by the provisions of article 23, of the said convention, deposited by their respective plenipotentiaries with the Government of Great Britain.

And whereas the Senate of the United States gave its advice and consent to the ratification of the said convention with the following understanding: "That nothing in the ninth article of the regulations affixed to the convention shall be deemed to exclude the United States from the execution of her inspection laws upon vessels entering in or clearing from her ports."

Now, therefore, be it known that I, Woodrow Wilson, President of the United States of America, have caused the said convention and annexes to be made public, to the end that the same and every article and clause thereof may be observed and fulfilled with good faith by the United States and the citizens thereof, subject to the said understanding.

In testimony whereof, I have hereunto set my hand and caused the seal of the United States to be affixed.

Done at the City of Washington this eighth day of July in the year of our Lord one thousand nine hundred and thirteen and of the Independence of the United [SEAL.] States of America the one hundred and thirty-eighth.

WOODROW WILSON.

By the President:

W. J. BRYAN,

Secretary of State.

Signed at London, July 5, 1912.

Ratification advised by the Senate, January 22, 1913.

Ratified by the President, February 5, 1913.

Ratification of the United States deposited with the Government of Great Britain February 20, 1913.

Proclaimed, July 8, 1913.

APPENDIX VI.

INTERNATIONAL RADIOTELEGRAPH CONVENTION, LONDON, 1912.

[Translation.]

International Radiotelegraph Convention concluded between Germany and the German Protectorates, the United States of America and the possessions of the United States of America, the Argentine Republic, Austria, Hungary, Bosnia-Herzegovina, Belgium, the Belgian Kongo, Brazil, Bulgaria, Chile, Denmark, Egypt, Spain and the Spanish Colonies, France and Algeria, French West Africa, French Equatorial Africa, Indo-China, Madagascar, Tunis, Great Britain and the various British Colonies and Protectorates, the Union of South Africa, the Australian Federation, Canada, British India, New Zealand, Greece, Italy and the Italian Colonies, Japan and Chosen, Formosa, Japanese Sakhalin and the leased territory of Kwantung, Morocco, Monaco, Norway, the Netherlands, the Dutch Indies and the Colony of Curaçao, Persia, Portugal and the Portuguese Colonies, Roumania, Russia and the Russian Possessions and Protectorates, the Republic of San Marino, Siam, Sweden, Turkey, and Uruguay.

The undersigned, plenipotentiaries of the Governments of the countries enumerated above, having met in conference at London, have agreed on the following convention, subject to ratification:

ARTICLE 1.

The high contracting parties bind themselves to apply the provisions of the present convention to all radio stations (both coastal stations and stations on shipboard) which are established or worked by the contracting parties and open to public service between the coast and vessels at sea.

They further bind themselves to make the observance of these provisions obligatory upon private enterprises authorized either to establish or work coastal stations for radiotelegraphy open to public service between the coast and vessels at sea, or to establish or work radio stations, whether open to general public service or not, on board of vessels flying their flag.

ARTICLE 2.

By "coastal stations" is to be understood every radio station established on shore or on board a permanently moored vessel used for the exchange of correspondence with ships at sea.

Every radio station established on board any vessel not permanently moored is called a "station on shipboard."

ARTICLE 3.

The coastal stations and the stations on shipboard shall be bound to exchange radiograms without distinction of the radio system adopted by such stations.

Every station on shipboard shall be bound to exchange radiograms with every other station on shipboard without distinction of the radio system adopted by such stations.

However, in order not to impede scientific progress, the provisions of the present Article shall not prevent the eventual employment of a radio system incapable of communicating with other systems, provided that such incapacity shall be due to the specific nature of such system and that it shall not be the result of devices adopted for the sole purpose of preventing intercommunication.

ARTICLE 4.

Notwithstanding the provisions of Article 3, a station may be reserved for a limited public service determined by the object of the correspondence or by other circumstances independent of the system employed.

ARTICLE 5.

Each of the High Contracting Parties undertakes to connect the coastal stations to the telegraph system by special wires, or, at least, to take other measures which will insure a rapid exchange between the coastal stations and the telegraph system.

ARTICLE 6.

The High Contracting Parties shall notify one another of the names of coastal stations and stations on shipboard referred to in Article 1, and also of all data, necessary to facilitate and accelerate the exchange of radiograms, as specified in the Regulations.

ARTICLE 7.

Each of the High Contracting Parties reserves the right to prescribe or permit at the stations referred to in Article 1, apart from the installation the data of which are to be published in conformity with Article 6, the installation and working of other devices for the purpose of establishing special radio communication without publishing the details of such devices.

ARTICLE 8.

The working of the radio stations shall be organized as far as possible in such manner as not to disturb the service of other radio stations.

ARTICLE 9.

Radio stations are bound to give absolutely priority to calls of distress from whatever source, to similarly answer such calls and to take such action with regard thereto as may be required.

ARTICLE 10.

The charge for a radiogram shall comprise, according to the circumstances:

1. (a) The coastal rate, which shall fall to the coastal station;

(b) The shipboard rate, which shall fall to the shipboard station.

2. The charge for transmission over the telegraph lines, to be computed according to the ordinary rules.

3. The charges for transit through the intermediate coastal or shipboard stations and the charges for special services requested by the sender.

The coastal rate shall be subject to the approval of the Government of which the coastal station is dependent, and the shipboard rate to the approval of the Government of which the ship is dependent.

ARTICLE 11.

The provisions of the present Convention are supplemented by Regulations, which shall have the same force and go into effect at the same time as the Convention.

The provisions of the present Convention and of the Regulations relating thereto may at any time be modified by the High Contracting Parties by common consent. Conferences of plenipotentiaries having power to modify the Convention and the Regulations, shall take place from time to time; each conference shall fix the time and place of the next meeting.

ARTICLE 12.

Such conferences shall be composed of delegates of the Governments of the contracting countries.

In the deliberations each country shall have but one vote.

If a Government adheres to the Convention for its colonies, possessions or protectorates, subsequent conferences may decide that such colonies, possessions or protectorates, or a part thereof, shall be considered as forming a country as regards the application of the preceding paragraph. But the number of votes at the disposal of one Government, including its colonies, possessions or protectorates, shall in no case exceed six.

The following shall be considered as forming a single country for the application of the present Article:

German East Africa.
German Southwest Africa.
Kamerun.
Togo Land.
German Protectorates in the Pacific.
Alaska.
Hawaii and the other American possessions in Polynesia.
The Philippine Islands.
Porto Rico and the American possessions in the Antilles.
The Panama Canal Zone.
The Belgian Congo.
The Spanish Colony of the Gulf of Guinea.
French East Africa.
French Equatorial Africa.
Indo-China.
Madagascar.
Tunis.
The Union of South Africa.
The Australian Federation.
Canada.
British India.
New Zealand.
Eritrea.
Italian Somaliland.
Chosen, Formosa, Japanese Sakhalin and the leased territory of Kwantung.
The Dutch Indies.
The Colony of Curaçao.
Portuguese West Africa.
Portuguese East Africa and the Portuguese possessions in Asia.
Russian Central Asia (littoral of the Caspian Sea).
Bokhara.
Khiva.
Western Siberia (littoral of the Arctic Ocean).
Eastern Siberia (littoral of the Pacific Ocean).

ARTICLE 13.

The International Bureau of the Telegraph Union shall be charged with collecting, coordinating and publishing information of every kind relating to radiotelegraphy, examining the applications for changes in the Convention or Regulations, promulgating the amendments adopted, and generally performing all administrative work referred to it in the interest of international radiotelegraphy.

The expense of such institution shall be borne by all the contracting countries.

ARTICLE 14.

Each of the High Contracting Parties reserves to itself the right of fixing the terms on which it will receive radiograms proceeding from or intended for any station, whether on shipboard or coastal, which is not subject to the provisions of the present Convention.

If a radiogram is received the ordinary rates shall be applicable to it.

Any radiogram proceeding from a station on shipboard and received by a coastal station of a contracting country, or accepted in transit by the administration of a contracting country, shall be forwarded.

Any radiogram intended for a vessel shall also be forwarded if the administration of the contracting country has accepted it originally or in transit from a non-contracting country, the coastal station reserving the right to refuse transmission to a station on shipboard subject to a non-contracting country.

ARTICLE 15.

The provisions of Articles 8 and 9 of this Convention are also applicable to radio installation other than those referred to in Article 1.

ARTICLE 16.

Governments which are not parties to the present Convention shall be permitted to adhere to it upon their request. Such adherence shall be communicated through diplomatic channels to the contracting Government in whose territory the last conference shall have been held, and by the latter to the remaining Governments.

The adherence shall carry with it to the fullest extent acceptance of all the clauses of this Convention and admission to all the advantages stipulated therein.

The adherence to the Convention by the Government of a country having colonies, possessions, or protectorates shall not carry with it the adherence of its colonies, possessions or protectorates unless a declaration to that effect is made by such Government. Such colonies, possessions, and protectorates, as a whole or each of them, separately, may form the subject of a separate adherence or a separate denunciation within the provisions of the present Article and of Article 22.

ARTICLE 17.[1]

The provisions of Articles 1, 2, 3, 5, 6, 7, 8, 11, 12 and 17 of the International Telegraph Convention of St. Petersburg of July 10–22, 1875, shall be applicable to international radiotelegraphy.

ARTICLE 18.

In case of disagreement between two or more contracting Governments regarding the interpretation or execution of the present Convention or of the Regulations referred to in Article 11, the question in dispute may, by mutual agreement, be submitted to arbitration. In such case each of the Governments concerned shall choose another Government not interested in the question at issue.

The decision of the arbiters shall be arrived at by the absolute majority of votes.

---

[1] See translation of articles of the International Telegraph Convention on p. 132.

In case of a division of votes, the arbiters shall choose, for the purpose of settling the disagreement, another contracting Government which is likewise a stranger to the question at issue. In case of failure to agree on a choice, each arbiter shall propose a disinterested contracting Government and lots shall be drawn between the Governments proposed. The drawing of the lots shall fall to the Government within whose territory the international bureau provided for in Article 13 shall be located.

ARTICLE 19.

The High Contracting Parties bind themselves to take, or propose to their respective legislatures, the necessary measures for insuring the execution of the present Convention.

ARTICLE 20.

The High Contracting Parties shall communicate to one another any laws already framed, or which may be framed, in their respective countries relative to the object of the present Convention.

ARTICLE 21.

The High Contracting Parties shall preserve their entire liberty as regards radio installations other than provided for in Article 1, especially naval and military installations, and stations used for communications between fixed points. All such installations and stations shall be subject only to the obligations provided for in Articles 8 and 9 of the present Convention.

However, when such installations and stations are used for public maritime service they shall conform, in the execution of such service, to the provisions of the Regulations as regards the mode of transmission and rates.

On the other hand, if coastal stations are used for general public service with ships at sea and also for communication between fixed points, such stations shall not be subject, in the execution of the last named service, to the provisions of the Convention except for the observance of Articles 8 and 9 of this Convention.

Nevertheless, fixed stations used for correspondence between land and land shall not refuse the exchange of radiograms with another fixed station on account of the system adopted by such station; the liberty of each country shall, however, be complete as regards the organization of the service for correspondence between fixed points and the nature of the correspondence to be effected by the stations reserved for such service.

ARTICLE 22.

The present Convention shall go into effect on the 1st day of July, 1913, and shall remain in force for an indefinite period or until the expiration of one year from the day when it shall be denounced by any of the contracting parties.

Such denunciation shall affect only the Government in whose name it shall have been made. As regards the other Contracting Powers, the Convention shall remain in force.

ARTICLE 23.

The present Convention shall be ratified and the ratifications exchanged at London with the least possible delay.

In case one or several of the High Contracting Parties shall not ratify the Convention, it shall nevertheless be valid as to the Parties which shall have ratified it.

In witness whereof the respective plenipotentiaries have signed one copy of the Convention, which shall be deposited in the archives of the British Government, and a copy of which shall be transmitted to each Party.

Done at London, July 5, 1912.

FINAL PROTOCOL.

[Translation.]

At the moment of signing the Convention adopted by the International Radiotelegraph Conference of London the undersigned plenipotentiaries have agreed as follows:

I.

The exact nature of the adherence notified on the part of Bosnia-Herzegovina not yet being determined, it is recognized that one vote shall be assigned to Bosnia-Herzegovina but that a decision will be necessary at a later date as to whether this vote belongs to Bosnia-Herzegovina in virtue of the second paragraph of Article 12 of the Convention, or whether this vote is accorded to it in conformity with the provisions of the third paragraph of that Article.

II.

Note is taken of the following declaration:

The Delegation of the United States declares that its government is under the necessity of abstaining from all action with regard to rates, because the transmission of radiograms as well as of ordinary telegrams in the United States is carried on, wholly or in part, by commercial or private companies.

III.

Note is likewise taken of the following declaration:

The Government of Canada reserves the right to fix separately, for each of its coastal stations, a total maritime rate for radiograms proceeding from North America and destined for any ship whatever, the coastal rate amounting to three-fifths and the shipboard rate to two-fifths of the total rate.

In witness whereof the respective plenipotentiaries have drawn up the present Final Protocol, which shall be of the same force and effect as though the provisions thereof had been embodied in the text of the Convention itself to which it has reference, and they have signed one copy of the same, which shall be deposited in the archives of the British Government, and a copy of which shall be transmitted to each of the Parties.

Done at London, July 5, 1912.

SERVICE REGULATIONS AFFIXED TO THE INTERNATIONAL RADIOTELEGRAPH CONVENTION, LONDON, 1912.

[Translation.]

1. Organization of Radio Stations.

ARTICLE I.

The choice of radio apparatus and devices to be used by the coastal stations and stations on shipboard shall be unrestricted. The installation of such stations shall as far as possible keep pace with scientific and technical progress.

ARTICLE II.

Two wave lengths, one of 600 meters and the other of 300 meters, are authorized for general public service. Every coastal station opened to such service shall be equipped in such manner as to be able to use these two wave lengths, one of which shall be designated as the normal wave length of the station. During the whole time that a coastal station is open it shall be in condition to receive calls according to its normal wave length. For the correspondence specified under paragraph 2 of Article XXXV, however, a wave length of 1800 meters shall be used. In addition, each Government may authorize in coastal stations the employment of other wave lengths designed to insure long-range service or any service other than for general public correspondence established in conformity with the provisions of the Convention under the reservation that such wave lengths do not exceed 600 meters or that they do exceed 1600 meters.

In particular, stations used exclusively for sending signals designed to determine the position of ships shall not employ wave lengths exceeding 150 meters.

ARTICLE III.

(1) Every station on shipboard shall be equipped in such manner as to be able to use wave lengths of 600 meters and of 300 meters. The first shall be the normal wave length and may not be exceeded for transmission except in the case referred to under Article XXXV (paragraph 2).

Other wave lengths, less than 600 meters, may be used in special cases and under the approval of the managements to which the coastal and shipboard stations concerned are subject.

(2) During the whole time that a station on shipboard is open it shall be able to receive calls according to its normal wave length.

(3) Vessels of small tonnage which are unable to use a wave length of 600 meters for transmission, may be authorized to employ exclusively the wave length of 300; they must be able to receive a wave length of 600 meters.

ARTICLE IV.

Communication between a coastal station and a station on shipboard shall be exchanged on the part of both by means of the same wave length. If, in a particular case, communication is difficult, the two stations may, by mutual consent, pass from the wave length with which they are communicating to the other regulation wave length. Both stations shall resume their normal wave length when the exchange of radiograms is finished.

ARTICLE V.

(1) The International Bureau shall draw up, publish, and revise from time to time an official chart showing the coastal stations, their normal ranges, the principal lines of navigation, and the time normally taken by ships for the voyage between the different ports of call.

(2) It shall draw up and publish a list of radio stations of the class referred to in Article I of the Convention, and from time to time supplements covering additions and modifications. Such list shall contain for each station the following data:

(a) In the case of coastal stations; name, nationality and geographical location indicated by the territorial subdivision and the latitude and longitude of the place; in the case of stations on shipboard; name and nationality of the ship; when the case arises, the name and address of the party working the station.

(b) The call letters (the calls shall be distinguishable from one another and each must be formed of a group of three letters).

(c) The normal range.

(d) The radio system with the characteristics of the transmitting system (musical sparks, tonality expressed by the number of double vibrations, etc.).

(e) The wave lengths used (the normal wave length to be underscored).

(f) The nature of the services carried on.

(g) The hours during which the station is open.

(h) When the case arises, the hour and method of transmitting time signals and meteorological telegrams.

(i) The coastal rate or shipboard rate.

(3) The list shall also contain such data relating to radio stations other than those specified in Article I of the Convention as may be communicated to the International Bureau by the management of the Radio Service ("administration") to which such stations are subject, provided that such managements are either adherents to the Convention or, if not adherents, have made the declaration referred to in Article XLVIII.

(4) The following notations shall be adopted in documents for use by the International Service to designate radio stations:

PG Station open to general public correspondence.

PR Station open to limited public correspondence.

P. Station of private interest.

O Station open exclusively to official correspondence.

N Station having continuous service.

X Station having no fixed working hours.

(5) The name of a station on shipboard appearing in the first column of the list shall be followed, in each case there are two or more vessels of the same name, by the call letters of such station.

ARTICLE VI.

The exchange of superfluous signals and words is prohibited to stations of the class referred to in Article I of the Convention. Experiments and practice will be permitted in such stations in so far as they do not interfere with the service of other stations.

Practice shall be carried on with wave lengths different from those authorized for public correspondence, and with the minimum of power necessary.

ARTICLE VII.

(1) All stations are bound to carry on the service with the minimum of energy necessary to insure safe communication.

(2) Every coastal or shipboard station shall comply with the following requirements:

(a) The waves sent out shall be as pure and as little damped as possible.

In particular, the use of transmitting devices in which the waves sent out are obtained by means of sparks directly in the aerial (plain aerial) shall not be authorized except in cases of distress.

It may, however, be permitted in the case of certain special stations (those of small vessels for example) in which the primary power does not exceed 50 watts.

(b) The apparatus shall be able to transmit and receive at a speed equal to at least 20 words a minute, words to be counted at the rate of 5 letters each.

New installations using more than 50 watts shall be equipped in such a way as to make it possible to obtain with ease several ranges less than the normal range, the shortest being approximately 15 nautical miles. Existing installations using more than 50 watts shall be remodeled, wherever possible, so as to comply with the foregoing provisions.

(c) Receiving apparatus shall be able to receive, with the greatest possible protection against interference, transmissions of the wave lengths specified in the present Regulations, up to 600 meters.

(3) Stations serving solely for determining the position of ships (radiophares) shall not operate over a radius greater than 30 nautical miles.

ARTICLE VIII.

Independently of the general requirements specified under Article VII, stations on shipboard shall likewise comply with the following requirements:

(a) The power transmitted to the radio apparatus, measured at the terminals of the generator of the station, shall not, under normal conditions, exceed one kilowatt.

(b) Subject to the provisions of Article XXXV, paragraph 2, power exceeding one kilowatt may be employed when the vessel finds it necessary to correspond while more than 200 nautical miles distant from the nearest coastal station, or when, owing to unusual circumstances, communication can be established only by means of an increase of power.

Article IX.

(1) No station on shipboard shall be established or worked by private enterprise without a license issued by the Government to which the vessel is subject.

Stations on board of ships having their port of registry in a colony, possession, or protectorate may be described as subject to the authority of such colony, possession, or protectorate.

(2) Every shipboard station holding a license issued by one of the contracting Governments shall be considered by the other Governments as having an installation fulfilling the requirements stipulated in the present Regulations.

Competent authorities of the countries at which the ship calls may demand the production of the license. In default of such production, these authorities may satisfy themselves as to whether the radio installations of the ship fulfill the requirements imposed by the present Regulations.

When the management of a radio service of a country is convinced by its working that a station on shipboard does not fulfill the requirements, it shall, in every case, address a complaint to the management of the radio service of the country to which such ship is a subject. The subsequent procedure, when necessary, shall be the same as that prescribed in Article XII, paragraph 2.

Article X.

(1) The service of the station on shipboard shall be carried on by a telegraph operator holding a certificate issued by the Government to which the vessel is subject, or, in case of necessity and for one voyage only, by some other adhering Government.

(2) There shall be two classes of certificates:

The first class certificate shall attest the professional efficiency of the operator as regards:

(a) Adjustment of the apparatus and knowledge of its functioning.

(b) Transmission and acoustic reception at the rate of not less than 20 words a minute.

(c) Knowledge of the regulations governing the exchange of radio correspondence.

The second class certificate may be issued to operators who are able to transmit and receive at a rate of only 12 to 19 words a minute but who, in other respects, fulfill the requirements mentioned above. Operators holding second class certificates may be permitted on:

(a) Vessels which use radiotelegraphy only in their own service and in the correspondence of their crews, fishing vessels in particular.

(b) All vessels, as substitutes, provided such vessels have on board at least *one* operator holding a first class certificate. However, on vessels classed under the first category indicated in Article XIII, the service shall be carried on by at least two telegraph operators holding first class certificates.

In the stations on shipboard, transmissions shall be made only by operators holding first or second class certificates except in cases of necessity where it would be impossible to conform to this provision.

(3) The certificate shall furthermore state that the Government has bound the operator to secrecy with regard to the correspondence.

(4) The radio service of the station on shipboard shall be under the superior authority of the commanding officer of the ship.

Article XI.

Ships provided with radio installations and classed under the first two categories indicated in Article XIII are bound to have radio installations for distress calls, all the elements of which shall be kept under conditions of the greatest possible safety to be determined by the Government issuing the license. Such emergency installations shall have their own source of energy, be capable of quickly being set into operation, of functioning for at least six hours, and have a minimum range of 80 nautical miles for ships of the first category and 50 miles for those of the second. Such emergency installations shall not be required in the case of vessels the regular installations of which fulfill the requirements of the present Article.

Article XII.

If the management of the radio service of a country has knowledge of any infraction of the Convention or of the Regulations committed in any of the stations authorized by it, it shall ascertain the facts and fix the responsibility.

In the case of stations on shipboard, if the operator is responsible for such infraction, the management of the radio service shall take the necessary measures, and, if the necessity should arise, withdraw the certificate. If it is ascertained that the infraction is the result of the condition of the apparatus or of instructions given the operator, the same method shall be pursued with regard to the license issued to the vessel.

(2) In cases of repeated infractions chargeable to the same vessel, if the representations made to the management of the country to which the vessel is subject by that of another country remain without effect, the latter shall be at liberty, after giving due notice, to authorize its coastal stations not to accept communications proceeding from the vessel at fault. In case of disagreement between the managements of the radio service of two countries, the question shall be submitted to arbitration at the request of either of the two Governments concerned. The procedure is indicated in Article 18 of the Convention.

2. Hours of Service of Stations.

Article XIII.

(1) Coastal stations:

(a) The service of coastal stations shall, as far as possible, be constant, day and night, without interruption.

Certain coastal stations, however, may have a service of limited duration. The management of the radio service of each country shall fix the hours of service.

(b) The coastal stations whose service is not constant shall not close before having transmitted all their radiograms to the vessels which are within their radius of action, nor before having received from such vessels all the radiograms of which notice has been given. This provision is likewise applicable when vessels signal their presence before the actual cessation of work.

(2) Stations on shipboard:

(a) Stations on shipboard shall be classed under three categories:

(1) Stations having constant service.

(2) Stations having a service of limited duration.

(3) Stations having no fixed working hours.

When the ship is under way, the following shipboard stations shall have an operator constantly listening in: First, stations of the first category; second, those of the second category during the hours in which they are open to service. During the remaining hours the last named stations shall have an operator at the radio instrument listening in during the first 10 minutes of each hour. Stations of the third category are not bound to perform any regular service of listening in.

It shall fall to the Governments issuing the licenses specified in Article IX to fix the category in which the ship shall be classed as regards its obligations in the matter of listening in. Mention shall be made of such classification in the license.

3. Form and Posting of Radiograms.

Article XIV.

(1) Radiograms shall show, as the first word of the preamble, that the service is "radio."

(2) In the transmission of radiograms proceeding from a ship at sea, the date and hour of posting at the shipboard station shall be stated in the preamble.

(3) Upon forwarding a radiogram over the telegraph system, the coastal station shall show thereon as the office of origin, the name of the ship of origin as it appears in the list, and also when the case arises, that of the last ship which acted as intermediary. Those data shall be followed by the name of the coastal station.

Article XV.

The address of radiograms intended for ships shall be as complete as possible.

It shall embrace the following:

(a) The name or title of the addressee, with additional designations, if any.

(b) The name of the vessel as it appears in the first column of the list.

(c) The name of the coastal station as it appears in the list.

The name of the ship, however, may be replaced, at the sender's risk, by the designation of the route to be followed by such vessel, as determined by the names of the ports of departure and destination or by any other equivalent information.

(2) In the address, the name of the ship as it appears in the first column of the list, shall, in all cases and independently of its length, be counted as one word.

(3) Radiograms framed with the aid of the International Code of Signals shall be transmitted to their destination without being translated.

4. Rates.

Article XVI.

(1) The coastal rate and the shipboard rate shall be fixed in accordance with the tariff per word, pure and simple, on the basis of an equitable remuneration for the radio work, with an optional minimum rate per radiogram.

The coastal rate shall not exceed 60 centimes (11.6 cents) a word, and the shipboard rate shall not exceed 40 centimes (7.7 cents) a word. However, each management shall be at liberty to authorize coastal and shipboard rates higher than such maxima in the case of stations of ranges exceeding 400 nautical miles, or of stations whose work is exceptionally difficult owing to physical conditions in connection with the installation or working of the same.

The optional minimum rate per radiogram shall not be higher than the coastal rate or shipboard rate for a radiogram of 10 words.

(2) In the case of radiograms proceeding from or destined for a country and exchanged directly with the coastal stations of such country, the rate applicable to the transmission over the telegraph lines shall not, on the average, exceed the inland rate of such country.

Such rate shall be computed per word, pure and simple, with an optional minimum rate which shall not exceed the rate for 10 words. It shall be stated in francs by the management of the radio service of the country to which the coastal station is subject.

In the case of countries of the European system, with the exception of Russia and Turkey, there shall be but one rate for the territory of each country.

ARTICLE XVII.

(1) When a radiogram proceeding from a ship and intended for the coast passes through one or two shipboard stations, the charges shall comprise, in addition to the rates of the shipboard station of origin, the coastal station and the telegraph lines, the shipboard rate of each of the ships which have participated in the transmission.

(2) The sender of a radiogram proceeding from the coast and intended for a ship may require that his message be transmitted by way of one or two stations on shipboard; he shall deposit for this purpose an amount equal to the radio and telegraph rates and, in addition, a sum to be fixed by the office of origin, as surety for the payment to the intermediary shipboard stations of the transit rates, fixed by Paragraph 1. He shall further pay, at his option, either the rate for a telegram of five words or the price of the postage on a letter to be sent by the coastal station to the office of origin giving the necessary information for the liquidation of the amounts deposited.

The radiogram shall then be accepted at the sender's risk; it shall show before the address the prepaid instruction, to wit: "X retransmissions telegraph" or "X retransmissions letter" according to whether the sender desired the information necessary for the liquidation of the deposits to be furnished by telegraph or by letter.

(3) The rate for radiograms proceeding from a ship intended for another ship, and forwarded through one or two intermediary coastal stations, shall comprise:

The shipboard rates of the two ships, the coastal rate of the coastal station or two coastal stations, as the case may be, and the telegraph rate, when necessary, applicable to the transmission between the two coastal stations.

(4) The rate for radiograms exchanged between ships without the intervention of a coastal station shall comprise the shipboard rates of the vessels of origin and destination together with the shipboard rates of the intermediary stations.

(5) The coastal and shipboard rates accruing to the stations of transit shall be the same as those fixed for such stations when they are stations of origin or destination. In no case shall they be collected more than once.

(6) In the case of every coastal station acting as intermediary, the rate to be collected for the service of transit shall be the highest coastal rate applicable to direct communication with the two ships concerned.

ARTICLE XVIII.

The country within whose territory a coastal station is established which serves as intermediary for the exchange of radiograms between a station on board ship and another country shall be considered, so far as the application of telegraph rates is concerned, as the country of origin or of destination of such radiograms, and not as the country of transit.

5. Collection of Charges.

ARTICLE XIX.

The total charge for radiograms shall be collected of the sender, with the exception of:

(a) Charges for special delivery (Art. LVIII, Par. 1, of the Telegraph Regulations);
(b) Charges applicable to inadmissible combinations or alterations of words noted by the office or station of destination (Art. XIX, Par. 9, of the Telegraph Regulations), such charges being collected of the addressee.

Stations on shipboard shall to that end have the necessary tariffs. They shall be at liberty, however, to obtain information from coastal stations on the subject of rates for radiograms for which they do not possess all the necessary data.

(2) The counting of words by the office of origin shall be conclusive in the case of radiograms intended for ships and that of the shipboard station of origin shall be conclusive in the case of radiograms proceeding from ships, both for purposes of trans-

mission and of the international accounts. However, when the radiogram is worded wholly or in part, either in one of the languages of the country of destination, in the case of radiograms proceeding from ships, or in one of the languages of the country to which the ship is subject, in the case of radiograms intended for ships, and contains combinations or alterations of words contrary to the usage of such language, the bureau or shipboard station of destination, as the case may be, shall have the right to recover from the addressee the amount of charge not collected. In case of refusal to pay, the radiogram may be withheld.

6. Transmission of Radiograms.

(A) SIGNALS OF TRANSMISSION.

ARTICLE XX.

The signals to be employed are those of the Morse International Code.

ARTICLE XXI.

Ships in distress shall use the following signal:

. . . — — — . . .

repeated at brief intervals, followed by the necessary particulars.

As soon as a station hears the signal of distress it shall cease all correspondence and not resume it until after it has made sure that the correspondence to which the call for assistance has given rise is terminated.

Stations which hear a signal of distress shall conform to the instructions given by the ship making such signal as regards the order of the messages or their cessation.

In case the call letters of a particular station are added at the end of the series of calls for assistance, the answer to the call shall be incumbent upon that station alone unless such station fails to reply. If the call for assistance does not specify any particular station, every station hearing such call shall be bound to answer it.

ARTICLE XXII.

For the purpose of giving or requesting information concerning the radio service, stations shall make use of the signals contained in the list appended to the present Regulations.

(B) ORDER OF TRANSMISSION.

ARTICLE XXIII.

Between two stations radiograms of the same order shall be transmitted one by one, by the two stations alternately, or in series of several radiograms, as the coastal station may indicate, provided the duration of the transmission of each series does not exceed 15 minutes.

(C) METHOD OF CALLING RADIO STATIONS AND TRANSMISSION OF RADIOGRAMS.

ARTICLE XXIV.

(1) As a general rule, it shall be the shipboard station that calls the coastal station whether it has radiograms to transmit or not.

(2) In waters where the radio traffic is very great (British Channel, etc.), a coastal station should not, as a general rule, be called by a shipboard station unless the former is within normal range of the shipboard station and not until the distance of the vessel from the coastal station is less than 75 per cent of the normal range of the latter.

(3) Before proceeding to call, the coastal station or the station on shipboard shall adjust its receiving apparatus to its maximum sensibility and make sure that no other correspondence is being carried on within its radius of action; if it finds other-

wise, it shall wait for the first pause, unless it is convinced that its call will not be likely to disturb the correspondence in progress. The same applies in case the station desires to answer a call.

(4) For calling, every station shall use the normal wave of the station it wishes to call.

(5) If in spite of these precautions the transmission of a radiogram is impeded at any place, the call shall cease upon the first request from a coastal station open to public correspondence. The latter station shall in such case indicate the approximate length of time it will be necessary to wait.

(6) The station on shipboard shall make known to every coastal station to which it has signaled its presence the moment at which it proposes to cease its operations and the probable duration of the interruption.

ARTICLE XXV.

(1) The call shall comprise the signal

— · — · —

the call letters of the station called transmitted three times, the word "from" (de) followed by the called letters of the sending station transmitted three times.

(2) The called station shall answer by making the signal

— · — · —

followed by the call letters of the corresponding station transmitted three times, the word "from," its own call letters, and the signal

— · — ·

(3) Stations desiring to enter into communication with ships, without, however, knowing the names of the ships within their radius of action, may employ the signal

— · — · — — · —

(signal of inquiry). The provisions of paragraphs 1 and 2 are likewise applicable to the transmission of a signal of inquiry and to the answer to such signal.

ARTICLE XXVI.

If a station called does not answer the call (Article XXV) transmitted three times at intervals of two minutes, the call shall not be resumed until after an interval of 15 minutes, the station issuing the call having first made sure of the fact that no radio correspondence is in progress.

ARTICLE XXVII.

Every station which has occasion to transmit a radiogram requiring the use of high power shall first send out three times the signal of warning — — · · — — with the minimum of power necessary to reach the neighboring stations. It shall not begin to transmit with high power until 30 seconds after sending the signal of warning.

ARTICLE XXVIII.

(1) As soon as the coastal station has answered, the shipboard station shall furnish it with the following data in case it has messages to transmit; such data shall likewise be furnished upon request from the coastal station:

(a) The approximate distance, in nautical miles, of the vessel from the coastal station.

(b) The position of the vessel indicated in a concise form and adapted to the circumstances of the case.

(c) Her next port of call.

(d) The number of radiograms, if they are of normal length, or the number of words, if the messages are unusually long.

The speed of the ship in nautical miles shall also be given if specially requested by the coastal station.

(2) The coastal station shall answer stating, as provided in paragraph 1, either the number of radiograms or the number of words to be transmitted to the ship, and also the order of transmission.

(3) If the transmission cannot take place immediately, the coastal station shall inform the station on shipboard of the approximate length of time that it will be necessary to wait.

(4) If a shipboard station called cannot receive for the moment, it shall inform the station calling of the approximate length of time that it will be necessary to wait.

(5) In the exchange of messages between two stations on shipboard, it shall fall to the station called to fix the order of transmission.

Article XXIX.

When a coastal station receives calls from several shipboard stations, it shall decide the order in which such stations shall be admitted to exchange their messages.

In fixing this order the coastal station shall be guided exclusively by the necessity of permitting each station concerned to exchange the greatest possible number of radiograms.

Article XXX.

Before beginning the exchange of correspondence the coastal station shall advise the shipboard station whether the transmission is to be effected in the alternate order or by series (Article XXIII); it shall then begin the transmission or follow up the preliminaries with the signal

— · —

Article XXXI.

The transmission of the radiogram shall be preceded by the signal

— · — · —

and terminated by the signal

· — · — ·

followed by the name of the sending station and by the signal

— · —

In the case of a series of radiograms, the name of the sending station and the signal — · — shall only be given at the end of the series.

Article XXXII.

When a radiogram to be transmitted contains more than 40 words, the sending station shall interrupt the transmission by the signal · · — — · · after each series of about 20 words and shall not resume it until after it has obtained from the receiving station a repetition of the last word duly received, followed by the said signal, or, if the reception is good, by the signal — · —

In the case of transmission by series, acknowledgment of receipt shall be made after each radiogram.

Coastal stations engaged in the transmission of long radiograms shall suspend the transmission at the end of each period of 15 minutes, and remain silent for a period of three minutes before resuming the transmission.

Coastal and shipboard stations working under the conditions specified in Article XXXV, Par. 2, shall suspend work at the end of each period of 15 minutes and listen in with a wave length of 600 meters during a period of three minutes before resuming the transmission.

Article XXXIII.

(1) When the signals become doubtful every possible means shall be resorted to to finish the transmission. To this end the radiogram shall be transmitted three times at most at the request of the receiving station. If in spite of such triple repetition the signals are still unreadable the radiogram shall be canceled.

If no acknowledgment of receipt is received the transmitting station shall again call up the receiving station. If no reply is made after three calls the transmission shall not be followed up any further. In such case the sending station shall have the privilege of obtaining the acknowledgment of receipt through the medium of another radio station, using, when necessary, the lines of the telegraph system.

(2) If in the opinion of the receiving station the radiogram, although imperfectly received, is nevertheless capable of transmission, said station shall enter the words "reception doubtful" at the end of the preamble and let the radiogram follow. In such case the management of the radio service of the country to which the coastal station is subject shall claim the charges in conformity with Article XLII of the present Regulations. If, however, the shipboard station subsequently transmits the radiogram to another coastal station of the same management, the latter can claim only the rates applicable to a single transmission.

(d) Acknowledgment of receipt and conclusion of work.

Article XXXIV.

(1) Receipt shall be acknowledged in the form prescribed by the International Telegraph Regulations; it shall be preceded by the call letters of the transmitting station and followed by those of the receiving station.

(2) The conclusion of a correspondence between two stations shall be indicated by each of the two stations by means of the signal

· · · — · —

followed by its own call letters.

(e) Directions to be followed in sending radiograms.

Article XXXV.

(1) In general, the shipboard stations shall transmit their radiograms to the nearest coastal station.

Nevertheless, if a shipboard station has the choice between several coastal stations at equal or nearly equal distances, it shall give the preference to the one established on the territory of the country of destination or normal transit for its radiograms.

(2) A sender on board a vessel shall, however, have the right to designate the coastal station through which he desires to have his radiogram transmitted. The station on shipboard shall then wait until such coastal station shall be the nearest.

In exceptional cases transmission may be made to a more distant coastal station, provided that:

(a) The radiogram is intended for the country in which such coastal station is situated and emanates from a ship subject to that country.

(b) Both stations use for calling and transmission a wave length of 1,800 meters.

(c) Transmission with this wave length does not interfere with a transmission made by means of the same wave length by a nearer coastal station.

(d) The station on shipboard is more than 50 nautical miles distant from any coastal station given in the list. The distance of 50 miles may be reduced to 25 miles provided the maximum power at the terminals of the generator does not exceed 5 kilowatts and that the stations on shipboard are established in conformity with Articles VII and VIII. This reduction in the distance shall not be admissible in the seas, bays or gulfs of which the shores belong to one country only and of which the opening to the high sea is less than 100 miles wide.

7. Delivery of Radiograms at Their Destination.

Article XXXVI.

When for any cause whatever a radiogram proceeding from a vessel at sea and intended for the coast cannot be delivered to the addressee, a notice of non-delivery shall be issued. Such notice shall be transmitted to the coastal station which received the original radiogram. The latter, after verifying the address, shall forward the notice to the ship, if possible, by the intervention, if need be, of another coastal station of the same country or of a neighboring country.

When a radiogram received by a shipboard station cannot be delivered, the station shall notify the office of the origin by official notice. In the case of radiograms emanating from the coast, such notice shall be transmitted, whenever practicable, to the coastal station through which the radiogram has passed in transit; otherwise, to another coastal station of the same country or of a neighboring country.

Article XXXVII.

If the ship for which a radiogram is intended has not signaled her presence to the coastal station within the period designated by the sender or, in the absence of such designation, by the morning of the 8th day following, the coastal station shall so notify the office of origin, which shall in turn inform the sender.

The latter shall have the right to ask, by a paid official notice, sent by either telegraph or mail and addressed to the coastal station, that his radiogram be held for a further period of 9 days for transmission to the vessel, and so on. In the absence of such request, the radiogram shall be put aside as not transmissible at the end of the 9th day (exclusive of the day of posting).

Nevertheless, if the coastal station is certain that the vessel has left its radius of action before it has been able to transmit the radiogram to her, such station shall immediately so notify the office of origin which shall without delay inform the sender of the cancellation of the message. The sender may, however, by a paid official notice, request the coastal station to transmit the radiogram the next time the vessel shall pass.

8. Special Radiograms.

Article XXXVIII.

The following radiograms only shall be accepted for transmission:

(1) Radiograms with answer prepaid. Such radiograms shall show before the address the indication "Answer prepaid" or "RP" supplemented by a statement of the amount paid in advance for the answer, thus: "Responsée Payée fr. x," or "RP fr. x."

The reply voucher issued by a station on shipboard shall carry with it the right to send, within the limits of its value, a radiogram to any destination whatever from the station on shipboard which has issued such voucher.

(2) Radiograms calling for repetition of message (for purposes of verification).

(3) Special delivery radiograms. Only, however, in cases where the amount of the charges for special delivery collected of the addressee. Countries which cannot accept such radiograms shall make a declaration to this effect to the International Bureau. Special delivery radiograms with charges collected of the sender may be accepted when they are intended for the country within whose territory the corresponding station is located.

(4) Radiograms to be delivered by mail.

(5) Multiple radiograms.

(6) Radiograms calling for acknowledgment of receipt. But only as regards notification of the date and hour at which the coastal station shall have transmitted to the station on shipboard the radiogram addressed to the latter.

(7) Paid service notices. Except those requesting a repetition or information. Nevertheless all paid service notices shall be accepted in transmission over the telegraph lines.

(8) Urgent radiograms. But only in transmission over the telegraph lines and subject to the application of the International Telegraph Regulations.

ARTICLE XXXIX.

Radiograms may be transmitted by a coastal station to a ship, or by a ship to another ship, with a view to being forwarded by mail from a port of call of the ship receiving the radiogram.

Such radiogram shall not be entitled to any radio retransmission.

The address of such radiogram shall embrace the following:

(1) The paid designation "mail" followed by the name of the port at which the radiogram is to be mailed.

(2) The name and complete address of the addressee.

(3) The name of the station on shipboard by which the radiogram is to be mailed.

(4) When necessary, the name of the coastal station.

Example: Mail Buenosaires 14 Calle Prat Valparaiso Avon Lizard.

The rate shall comprise, in addition to the radio and telegraph rates, a sum of 25 centimes (.048 cent) for the postage on the radiogram.

9. **Files.**

ARTICLE XL.

The originals of radiograms, together with the documents relating thereto retained by the managements of the radio service, shall be kept, with all the necessary precautions as regards secrecy, for a period of at least 15 months, beginning with the month following that of the posting of the radiogram.

Such originals and documents shall, as far as practicable, be sent at least once a month by the shipboard stations to the management of the radio service to which they are subject.

10. **Rebates and Reimbursements.**

ARTICLE XLI.

(1) With regard to rebates and reimbursements, the International Telegraph Regulations shall be applicable, taking into account the restrictions specified in Articles XXXVIII and XXXIX of the present Regulations and subject to the following reservations:

The time employed in the transmission of radiograms and the time that radiograms remain in a coastal station in the case of radiograms intended for ships, or in the station on shipboard in the case of radiograms proceeding from ships, shall not be counted as delays as regards rebates or reimbursements.

If the coastal station notifies the office of origin that a radiogram cannot be transmitted to the ship addressed, the management of the radio service of the country of origin shall immediately instigate reimbursement to the sender of the coastal and shipboard rates relating to the radiogram. In such case, the refunded charges shall not enter into the accounts provided for by Article XLII, but the radiogram shall be mentioned therein as a memorandum.

Reimbursements shall be borne by the different managements of the radio service and private enterprises which have taken part in the transmission of the radiogram, each management or private enterprise relinquishing its share of the rate. Radiograms to which Articles 7 and 8 of the Convention of St. Petersburg are applicable shall remain subject, however, to the provisions of the International Telegraph Regulations, except when the acceptance of such radiograms is the result of an error made by the telegraph service.

(2) When the acknowledgment of receipt of a radiogram has not reached the station which has transmitted the message, the charges shall be refunded only if the fact has been established that the radiogram is entitled to reimbursement.

11. Accounts and Payment of Charges.

Article XLII.

(1) The coastal and shipboard charges shall not enter into the accounts provided for by the International Telegraph Regulations.

The accounts regarding such charges shall be liquidated by the managements of the radio service of the countries concerned. They shall be drawn up by the radio managements to which the coastal stations are subject, and communicated by them to the radio managements concerned. In cases where the working of the coastal stations is independent of the management of the radio service of the country, the party working such stations may be substituted, as regards the accounts, for the radio management of such country.

(2) For transmission over the telegraph lines radiograms shall be treated, so far as the payment of rates is concerned, in conformity with the International Telegraph Regulations.

(3) For radiograms proceeding from ships, the radio management to which the coastal station is subject shall charge the radio management to which the shipboard station of origin is subject with the coastal and ordinary telegraph rates, the total charges collected for answers prepaid, the coastal and telegraph rates collected for repetition of message (for purposes of verification), charges relating to special delivery (in the case provided for in Article XXXVIII), or delivery by mail, and those collected for additional copies (TM). The radio management to which the coastal station is subject shall credit, when the case arises, through the channel of the telegraph accounts and through the medium of the offices which have participated in the transmission of the radiograms, the radio management to which the office of destination is subject with the total charges relating to answers prepaid. With respect to the telegraph rates and the charges relating to special delivery or delivery by mail, and to additional copies, the procedure shall be as prescribed in the Telegraph Regulations, the coastal station being considered as the telegraph office of origin.

For radiograms intended for a country lying beyond the country to which the coastal station belongs, the telegraph charges to be liquidated in conformity with the above provisions shall be those which result either from tables "A" and "B" annexed to the International Telegraph Regulations, or from special arrangements concluded between the radio managements of adjacent countries and published by such managements, and not the charges which might be collected in accordance with the special provisions of Articles XXIII, Par. 1, and XXVII, Par. 1, of the Telegraph Regulations.

For radiograms and paid service notices intended for ships, the radio management to which the office of origin is subject shall be charged directly by that to which the coastal station is subject with the coastal and shipboard rates. However, the total charges relating to answers prepaid shall be credited, if there is occasion, from country to country, through the channel of the telegraph accounts, until they reach the radio management to which the coastal station is subject. As regards the telegraph charges and the charges relating to delivery by mail and additional copies, the procedure shall be as prescribed in the Telegraph Regulations. The radio management to which the coastal station is subject shall credit that to which the ship of destination is subject with the shipboard rate, if there is occasion, with the rates accruing to the intermediary shipboard stations, the total charge collected for answers prepaid, the shipboard rates for repetition of message (for purposes of verification), and the charges collected for the preparation of additional copies and for delivery by mail.

Paid service notices and answers prepaid shall be treated in the radio accounts in all respects the same as other radiograms.

For radiograms transmitted by means of one or two intermediary stations on shipboard, each one of such stations shall charge the shipboard station of origin, in the case of a radiogram proceeding from a ship, or that of destination, in the case of a radiogram intended for a ship, with the shipboard rate accruing to it for transit.

(4) In general, the liquidation of accounts relating to correspondence between stations on shipboard shall be effected directly between the companies working such stations, the station of origin being charged by the station of destination.

(5) The monthly accounts serving as a basis for the special accounts of radiograms shall be made out for each radiogram separately with all the necessary data within a period of six months from the month to which they refer.

(6) The Governments reserve the right to enter into special agreements among themselves and with private companies (parties operating radio stations, shipping companies, etc.) with a view of adopting other provisions with regard to accounts.

12. International Bureau.

Article XLIII.

The additional expenses resulting from the work of the International Bureau so far as radio telegraphy is concerned shall not exceed 80,000 francs a year, exclusive of the special expenses arising from the convening of the International Conference.

The managements of the radio service of the contracting states shall, so far as contribution to the expenses is concerned, be divided into six classes, as follows:

1st Class:

Union of South Africa; Germany, United States of America; Alaska; Hawaii; and the other American possessions in Polynesia; Philippine Islands; Porto Rico and the American possessions in the Antilles; Panama Canal Zone; Argentine Republic; Australia; Austria; Brazil; Canada; France; Great Britain; Hungary; British India; Italy; Japan; New Zealand; Russia; Turkey.

2d Class:

Spain.

3d Class:

Russian Central Asia (littoral of the Caspian Sea); Belgium; Chile; Chosen; Formosa; Japanese Sakhalin and the leased territory of Kwantung; Dutch Indies; Norway; Netherlands; Portugal; Roumania; Western Siberia (littoral of the Arctic Ocean); Eastern Siberia (littoral of the Pacific Ocean); Sweden.

4th Class:

German East Africa; German Southwest Africa; Kamerun; Togo Land; German Protectorates in the Pacific; Denmark; Egypt; Indo-China; Mexico; Siam; Uruguay.

5th Class:

French West Africa; Bosnia-Herzegovina; Bulgaria; Greece; Madagascar; Tunis.

6th Class:

French Equatorial Africa; Portuguese West Africa; Portuguese East Africa and the Portuguese possessions in Asia; Bokhara; Belgian Kongo; Colony of Curaçao; Spanish Colony of the Gulf of Guinea; Eritrea; Khiva; Morocco; Monaco; Persia; San Marino, Italian Somaliland.

ARTICLE XLIV.

The management of the radio service of the different countries shall forward to the International Bureau a table in conformity with the annexed blank, containing the data enumerated in said table for stations such as referred to in Article V of the Regulations. Changes occurring and additional data shall be forwarded by the radio managements to the International Bureau between the 1st and 10th day of each month. With the aid of such data the International Bureau shall draw up the list provided for in Article V. The list shall be distributed to the radio managements concerned. The list and the supplements thereto may also be sold to the public at the cost price.

The International Bureau shall see to it that the same call letters for several radio stations shall not be adopted.

13. Meteorological Radiograms, Time Signals and Other Radiograms.

ARTICLE XLV.

(1) The managements of the radio service shall take the necessary steps to supply their coastal stations with meteorological radiograms containing indications concerning the district of such stations. Such radiograms, the text of which shall not exceed 20 words, shall be transmitted to ships upon request. The rate for such meteorological radiograms shall be carried to the account of the ships to which they are addressed.

(2) Meteorological observations made by certain vessels designated for this purpose by the country to which they are subject, may be transmitted once a day, as paid service notices, to the coastal stations authorized to receive the same by the managements concerned, who shall likewise designate the meteorological offices to which such observations shall be addressed by the coastal stations.

(3) Time signals and meteorological radiograms shall be transmitted one after the other in such a way that the total time occupied in their transmission shall not exceed 10 minutes. As a general rule, all radio stations whose transmissions might interfere with the reception of such signals and radiograms, shall remain silent during their transmission in order that all stations desiring it may be able to receive the same. Exception shall be made in cases of distress calls and of state telegrams.

(4) The managements of the radio service shall give to agencies of maritime information such data regarding losses and casualties at sea or other information of general interest to navigation, as the coastal stations may properly report.

14. Miscellaneous Provisions.

ARTICLE XLVI.

The exchange of correspondence between shipboard stations shall be carried on in such a manner as not to interfere with the service of the coastal stations, the latter, as a general rule, being accorded the right of priority for the public service.

ARTICLE XLVII.

Coastal stations and stations on shipboard shall not be bound to participate in the retransmission of radiograms except in cases where direct communication cannot be established between the stations of origin and destination.

The number of such transmissions shall, however, be limited to two.

In the case of radiograms intended for the coast, retransmission shall take place for the purpose of reaching the nearest coastal station.

Retransmission shall in every case be subject to the condition that the intermediate station which receives the radiogram in transit is in a position to forward it.

Article XLVIII.

If the route of a radiogram is partly over telegraph lines, or through radio stations subject to a non-contracting Government, such radiograms may be transmitted provided the managements of the radio service to which such lines or stations are subject have declared that, if the occasion should arise, they will comply with such provisions of the Convention and of the Regulations as are indispensable to the regular transmission of radiograms and that the payment of charges is insured. Such declaration shall be made to the International Bureau and communicated to the offices of the Telegraph Union.

Article XLIX.

Modifications of the present regulations which may be rendered necessary in consequence of the decisions of subsequent Telegraph Conferences shall go into effect on the date fixed for the application of the provisions adopted by each one of such conferences.

Article L.

The provisions of the International Telegraph Regulations shall be applicable analogously to radio correspondence in so far as they are not contrary to the provisions of the present regulations. The following provisions of the Telegraph Regulations, in particular, shall be applicable to radio correspondence: Article XXVII, paragraphs 3 to 6, relating to the collection of charges; Articles XXVI and XLI relating to the indication of the route to be followed; Article LXXV, paragraph 1, LXXVIII, paragraphs 2 to 4, and LXXIX, paragraphs 2 and 4, relating to the preparation of accounts. However: (1) The period of six months provided by paragraph 2 of Article LXXIX of the Telegraph Regulations for the verification of accounts shall be extended to nine months in the case of radiograms; (2) The provisions of Article XVI, paragraph 2, shall not be considered as authorizing gratuitous transmission, through radio stations, of service telegrams relating exclusively to the telegraph service, nor the free transmission over the telegraph lines of service telegrams relating exclusively to the radio service; (3) The provisions of Article LXXIX, paragraphs 3 and 5, shall not be applicable to radio accounts. As regards the application of the provisions of the Telegraph Regulations, coastal stations shall be considered as offices of transit except when the Radio Regulations expressly stipulate that such stations shall be considered as offices of origin or of destination.

In conformity with Article 11 of the Convention of London, the present Regulations shall go into effect on the first day of July, 1913.

In witness whereof the respective plenipotentiaries have signed one copy of these Regulations, which shall be deposited in the archives of the British Government, and a copy of which shall be transmitted to each of the Parties.

29732°—14——9

(Supplement to Article XLIV of the Regulations.)

Radio Management of . . . . Service Particulars of Radio Stations.

(a) COASTAL STATIONS.

Name.	Nationality.	Geographical location: E. East longitude. O. West longitude. N. North latitude. S. South latitude. Territorial subdivisions.	Call letters.	Normal range in nautical miles.	Radio system with the characteristics of the transmitting system.	Wave lengths in meters (the normal wave length to be underscored).	Nature of service furnished.	Hours during which station is open (local standard time).	Coastal rate, per word in francs, minimum rate per radiogram, in francs.	Remarks. (When necessary hour and manner of sending time signals and meteorological radiograms.)

(b) SHIPBOARD STATIONS.

Name.	Nationality.	Call letters.	Normal range in nautical miles.	Radio system with the characteristics of the transmitting system.	Wave lengths in meters.	Nature of service furnished.	Hours during which the station is open.	Shipboard rate per word in francs, minimum rate per radiogram in francs (1) War vessels (2) Merchant vessels.	Remarks. (When necessary name and address of the party working the station.)

(Supplement to Article XXII of the Regulations.)

List of Abbreviations to be used in Radio Communications.

Abbreviation.	Question.	Answer or notice.
—·—· ——·—	(C Q)	Signal of enquiry made by a station desiring to communicate.
— ·—·	(T R)	Signal announcing the sending of particulars concerning a station on shipboard (Art. XXII).
——··——	(!).........................	Signal indicating that a station is about to send at high power.
PRB	Do you wish to communicate by means of the International Signal Code?	I wish to communicate by means of the International Signal Code.
QRA	What ship or coast station is that?	This is....

List of Abbreviations to be used in Radio Communications—Continued.

Abbreviation.	Question.	Answer or notice.
QRB	What is your distance?	My distance is....
QRC	What is your true bearing?	My true bearing is....degrees.
QRD	Where are you bound for?	I am bound for....
QRF	Where are you bound from?	I am bound from....
QRG	What line do you belong to?	I belong to the....line.
QRH	What is you wave length in meters?	My wave length is....meters.
QRJ	How many words have you to send?	I have....words to send.
QRK	How do you receive me?	I am receiving well.
QRL	Are you receiving badly? Shall I send 20 · · · — · for adjustment?	I am receiving badly. Please send 20 · · · — · for adjustment.
QRM	Are you being interfered with?	I am being interfered with.
QRN	Are the atmospherics strong?	Atmospherics are very strong.
QRO	Shall I increase power?	Increase power.
QRP	Shall I decrease power?	Decrease power.
QRQ	Shall I send faster?	Send faster.
QRS	Shall I send slower?	Send slower.
QRT	Shall I stop sending?	Stop sending.
QRU	Have you anything for me?	I have nothing for you.
QRV	Are you ready?	I am ready. All right now.
QRW	Are you busy?	I am busy (or, I am busy with....). Please do not interfere.
QRX	Shall I stand by?	Stand by. I will call you when required.
QRY	When will be my turn?	Your turn will be No. ....
QRZ	Are my signals weak?	Your signals are weak.
QSA	Are my signals strong?	Your signals are strong.
QSB	Is my tone bad?	The tone is bad.
	Is my spark bad?	The spark is bad.
QSC	Is my spacing bad?	Your spacing is bad.
QSD	What is your time?	My time is....
QSF	Is transmission to be in alternate order or in series?	Transmission will be in alternate order.
QSG		Transmission will be in series of 5 messages.
QSH		Transmission will be in series of 10 messages.
QSJ	What rate shall I collect for....?	Collect....
QSK	Is the last radiogram canceled?	The last radiogram is canceled.
QSL	Did you get my receipt?	Please acknowledge.
QSM	What is your true course?	My true course is....degrees.
QSN	Are you in communication with land?	I am not in communication with land.
QSO	Are you in communication with any ship or station (or: with....)?	I am in communication with.... (through....).
QSP	Shall I inform....that you are calling him?	Inform....that I am calling him.
QSQ	Is....calling me?	You are being called by....
QSR	Will you forward the radiogram?	I will forward the radiogram.
QST	Have you received the general call?	General call to all stations.
QSU	Please call me when you have finished (or: at....o'clock).	Will call when I have finished.
QSV[1]	Is public correspondence being handled?	Public correspondence is being handled. Please do not interfere.
QSW	Shall I increase my spark frequency?	Increase your spark frequency.
QSY	Shall I send on a wave length of....meters?	Let us change to the wave length of....meters.
QSX	Shall I decrease my spark frequency?	Decrease your spark frequency.

[1] Public correspondence is any radio work, official or private, handled on commercial wave lengths.

When an abbreviation is followed by a mark of interrogation, it refers to the question indicated for that abbreviation.

EXAMPLES.

Station A. QRA?..........................What is the name of your station?

Station B. QRA Campania..............This is the Campania.

Station A. QRG?..........................To what line do you belong?

Station B. QRG Cunard QRZ...........I belong to the Cunard Line. Your signals are weak.

Station A then increases the power of its transmitter and sends:

Station A. QRK?..........................How are you receiving?

Station B. QRK...........................I am receiving well.

QRB 80.........................The distance between our stations is 80 nautical miles.

QRC 62.........................My true bearing is 62 degrees, etc.

EXTRACT FROM THE INTERNATIONAL TELEGRAPH CONVENTION, SIGNED AT ST. PETERSBURG, JULY 10-22, 1875.

(See Article 17 of the Convention, page 111.)

ARTICLE 1. The High Contracting Parties concede to all persons the right to correspond by means of the international telegraphs.

ART. 2. They bind themselves to take all the necessary measures for the purpose of insuring the secrecy of the correspondence and its safe transmission.

ART. 3. They declare, nevertheless, that they accept no responsibility as regards the international telegraph service.

ART. 5. Telegrams are classed in three categories:

(1) State telegrams: those emanating from the Head of the Nation, the Ministers, the Commanders-in-Chief of the Army and Naval forces, and the Diplomatic or Consular Agents of the Contracting Governments, as well as the answers to such telegrams.

(2) Service telegrams: those which emanate from the Managements of the Telegraph Service of the Contracting States and which relate either to the international telegraph service or to subjects of public interest determined jointly by such Managements.

(3) Private telegrams.

In the transmission, the State telegrams shall have precedence over other telegrams.

ART. 6. State telegrams and service telegrams may be issued in secret language, in any communications.

Private telegrams may be exchanged in secret language between two States which admit of this mode of correspondence.

The States which do not admit of private telegrams in secret language upon the expedition or arrival of the same, shall allow them to pass in transit, except in the case of suspension defined in Article 8.

ART. 7. The High Contracting Parties reserve the right to stop the transmission of any private telegram which may appear dangerous to the safety of the State, or which may be contrary to the laws of the country, to public order or good morals.

ART. 8. Each Government also reserves the right to suspend the international telegraph service for an indefinite period, if deemed necessary by it, either generally, or only over certain lines and for certain classes of correspondence, of which such Government shall immediately notify all the other Contracting Governments.

ART. 11. Telegrams relating to the international telegraph service of the Contracting States shall be transmitted free of charge over the entire systems of such States.

ART. 12. The High Contracting Parties shall render accounts to one another of the charges collected by each of them.

ART. 17. The High Contracting Parties reserve respectively the right to enter among themselves into special arrangements of any kind with regard to points of the service which do not interest the States generally.

INDEX.

○

Zeitfracht Medien GmbH
Ferdinand-Jühlke-Straße 7
99095 Erfurt, Deutschland
produktsicherheit@kolibri360.de